PRAISE F...
MAKE EVERY MOVE A MEDITATION

"Let me say it simply. Someone should have written this book a long time ago. Thanks, Nita. Systematically exercising consciousness while you systematically exercise the body in which it dwells...That's a major life hack. It's a way to work smart that's ideal for busy, modern people committed to a sound mind in a sound body."

—**Shinzen Young, meditation teacher, neuroscience research consultant, founder of Unified Mindfulness, and author of *Meditation in the Zone* and *The Science of Enlightenment***

"Humans evolved to survive predators and to find food, shelter, and mates. Those activities required noticing and responding to the subtlest unfoldings of nature. Now lost in a speed-and-greed world, we need to be reminded of who we are and why we are here. Nita Sweeney's *Make Every Move a Meditation* provides us exactly that, a deeply considered, well-organized, and beautifully presented guidebook back to self-actualization, flourishing, happiness, and meaning—an important work for every seeker."

—**Yun Rou, Daoist Monk, Tai Chi Master, and author of *The Monk of Park Avenue***

"Awakening awareness in the body is the portal to resting in an openhearted and dynamic presence. *Make Every Move a Meditation* is an accessible and powerful guide for taking our practice off the cushion and connecting deeply with the creativity, wisdom and aliveness that is our very essence."

—**Tara Brach, author of *Trusting the Gold***

"You exercise but don't have time to meditate? Or meditate but don't have time to exercise? Or maybe you would like to meditate but can't sit still. This book has the solution: Do both at once! Drawing from decades of experience in formal meditation settings, as well as many years as a long-distance runner, Nita Sweeney presents invaluable guidance toward bringing meditation into movement and making movement your practice. Highly recommended for anyone who moves, or sits still: in other words, everyone!"

—Sean Tetsudo Murphy, Sensei, Zen teacher in the White Plum
American Zen lineage, author of *One Bird, One Stone:*
108 Contemporary Zen Stories

"I love to walk and I'm a forty-five-year veteran of meditation, but I have never combined the two. Thanks to this book, that's about to change. I've been sharing meditation with others for the better part of two decades and teaching professionally for over ten years. Many times, students have asked me how to do moving meditations, and I've never had a good answer. Now I do. My answer is, 'Buy Nita Sweeney's book, *Make Every Move a Meditation.*' "

—Kim Colegrove, author of *Mindfulness for Warriors*
and owner of Pause First Academy

"I've been a regular runner and occasional meditator for years, but it never occurred to me to combine my meditation practice with my running routine. The two disciplines complement each other brilliantly. After reading Nita Sweeney's *Make Every Move a Meditation*, I look forward to many miles of meditative movement in the years to come."

—Denny Krahe, running coach, author of *Be Ready on Race Day*
and host of the *Diz Runs* podcast

"*Make Every Move A Meditation* is a gift for anyone seeking to incorporate meditation and mindfulness into their daily life. The author writes from her many years of personal practice and encourages us with advice that is clear, practical, and warmhearted. Nita Sweeney not only talks the talk but walks the walk (and runs the run!), offering the fruits of her experience to guide others along the path."

—Tania Casselle, MA Transpersonal Psychotherapy, award-winning writer, contemplative writing retreat leader, and senior faculty for Sage Institute for Creativity and Consciousness

"I don't practice mindfulness to get better at sitting still in quiet rooms. I practice to inhabit my life more fully. *Make Every Move a Meditation* encourages you to develop liberating attentional skills with your eyes open and your body moving. In it, Nita Sweeney shares practical strategies she's field-tested over the years and how they've equipped her to respond more effectively to a range of obstacles. She'll inspire you to expand your exploration of mindful awareness and to sneak it into more areas of your life."

—Daron Larson, mindfulness speaker, teacher, coach, and creator of the TEDxColumbus Talk: "Don't Try to Be Mindful"

MAKE EVERY MOVE A MEDITATION

MORE BOOKS BY NITA SWEENEY

Depression Hates a Moving Target:
How Running with My Dog Brought Me Back from the Brink

You Should Be Writing:
A Journal of Inspiration and Instruction to Keep Your Pen Moving
(co-created with Brenda Knight)

MAKE EVERY
MOVE A
MEDITATION

Mindful Movement
for Mental Health,
Well-Being, and Insight

BY NITA SWEENEY

CORAL GABLES

Cover Design: Morgane Leoni
Cover Illustration: Liliia/Adobe Stock
Layout & Design: Katia Mena

For permission requests, please contact the publisher at:
Mango Publishing Group
2850 S Douglas Road, 4th Floor
Coral Gables, FL 33134 USA
info@mango.bz

For special orders, quantity sales, course adoptions and corporate sales, please email the publisher at sales@mango.bz. For trade and wholesale sales, please contact Ingram Publisher Services at customer.service@ingramcontent.com or +1.800.509.4887.

Make Every Move a Meditation: Mindful Movement for Mental Health, Well-Being, and Insight

Library of Congress Cataloging-in-Publication number: 2022937304
ISBN: (print) 978-1-64250-989-2 , (ebook) 978-1-64250-990-8
BISAC category code REL007040, RELIGION / Buddhism / Theravada

Printed in the United States of America

To my many teachers, including:

Natalie Goldberg
Shinzen Young
Bhante Gunaratana
Sean Tetsudo Murphy, Sensei
Lama Jacqueline Mandell
Marcia Rose
Katherine and Danny Dreyer

And my first teacher, Ed,
who advised, "Try not to fidget."

CONTENTS

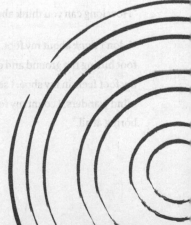

INTRODUCTION

On a bright Saturday morning, as I ran along the Olentangy Trail with three
other members of our pace group, the conversation turned to meditation. It
might as easily have turned to which central Ohio restaurant we would go to
for breakfast, upcoming races, or last week's Buckeye football game. Instead,
a woman asked how I practice.

"I do *sitting* meditation," I said. "But I also meditate while I run. I was
meditating just now."

"That's a thing?" another woman asked.

"It is for me." I explained.

"Today, I'm noticing my left foot. When my mind wanders, I gently
bring it back."

"The whole run?"

"Most of it."

"How long can you think about your foot? Isn't that boring?"

"I don't *think* about my foot. I experience it. I notice the sensation of my
foot hitting the ground and observe any changes. I pay attention to how
my foot feels in my shoe. I sense if it hits harder than my right. When my
mind wanders, I count my footfalls. When I pay close attention, it's not
boring at all."

Silence.

Eventually, someone brought up breakfast.

But a few weeks later, the woman who initially asked approached me. "I tried your left foot meditation. It's interesting. I rarely pay attention to my feet. Since I tried it, I feel more relaxed when I run." She thanked me.

That brief conversation led to this book. The woman, like many other people I've talked to, found the notion of movement meditation odd but also appealing. Movement meditation was worth exploring and explaining. Of course, I didn't create movement meditation; centuries-old traditions embrace it. But for that woman, it was new.

What I didn't tell my sister runner was that this path of noticing—whether it be her left foot, her breath, or her thinking—is about much more than physical activity.

Meditation might make her a better runner, or make someone else a better golfer, tennis player, dancer, gymnast, or weight lifter, but more importantly, consistent practice could lead her to insight—the kind that can enhance daily life. It might even free her from suffering, a pain she might not even know she has. If one person finds that, it will be worth any effort.

CHAPTER 1

WHY BOTHER?

If you're like most people, including me, you exercise for a variety of reasons. You're depressed, so you exercise to cheer up, or you're anxious and want to calm down. Maybe you hope to relax or zone out. Perhaps you seek bliss and joy, an escape from your troubles. Or you want to feel strong. Then again, you might just want to look fabulous in your swimsuit. No shame in that. The beach beckons.

Plus, you're already busy. There's the partner and the kids and the dog. You need to mow the lawn. That work project is (still) due, and those groceries aren't going to shop for themselves.

So why add what sounds like another task? Your mind gets a workout every day, all day long. Isn't exercise a time to give it a rest? Why pile what seems like another layer on top of your current exercise routine?

After all, meditation of any sort takes time, energy, grit, determination, and discipline. As contemporary Buddhist Monk Bhante Gunaratana (Bhante G.) says in *Mindfulness in Plain English*, "Meditation takes gumption."[1] Why on Earth would you want to infuse your movement with something that requires effort and dedication?

---

1   Ven. Henepola Gunaratana, *Mindfulness in Plain English* (Boston: Wisdom Publications, 1993), 7.

There are a host of reasons.

You're probably already aware of the many ways movement improves your life. Meditation enhances that. Studies on people who meditate show the physical, emotional, and cognitive benefits ranging from improved athletic performance to growing new brain cells.[2] Combine the two for a supercharged growth recipe.

But there's an even more compelling reason to add meditation to your movement routine.

Freedom.

Beneath any desire you may have to relax, zone out, or toughen up, and under that wish to look and feel physically and mentally better, lies the urge for freedom.

Freedom from what?

Freedom from suffering.

And that—freedom from suffering—is the main reason I bother.

During the winter after I turned forty-nine, a social media post by a high school friend caught my attention.

It read: "Call me crazy, but this running is getting to be fun!"

I did indeed think she was crazy, but she also looked like she was having fun.

I was definitely not having fun.

The chronic depression that had plagued me most of my life resurfaced after seven loved ones, including my twenty-four-year-old niece and my mother, all died during the same year. That friend's social media post found

---

2   Patrick Zeis "30 Evidence-Based Benefits of Meditation" www.balancedachievement. com/areas-of-life/benefits-of-meditation.

me on the couch. I don't remember bonbons specifically, but excess food had become the anchor in my "wellness plan," causing my weight to balloon. Exercise seemed long behind me, and I didn't believe it would help anyway. I was suffering so much; I wasn't sure I wanted to stay on the planet.

Meanwhile, that high school friend kept running.

As I watched her gradual progress, principles I knew from years of meditation and previous stints of movement resurfaced. The change in her and the shift I felt was familiar: impermanence. Her progress and my interest reflected the natural ebb and flow that's always happening, which many of us never notice.

Her online training plan said, "Sixty seconds of jogging." That's not all it said, but that phrase stuck like a mantra. As winter wore on, my curiosity grew.

One March weekday when my husband, Ed, and most of the neighbors were at work, I pulled on faded, tight workout clothes, picked up a digital kitchen timer, leashed up our yellow Labrador retriever, Morgan, and walked to a secluded ravine in our neighborhood where no one could see us. I set the timer for sixty seconds, then stood long enough for the dog to wander away and "water" a nearby shrub. When I finally hit the timer button, it set in motion a series of changes so huge I can hardly believe them myself.

But running was tough.

In my first book, a running and mental health memoir called *Depression Hates a Moving Target*, I shared how a congenital ankle defect, my weight, one especially unhelpful medical professional, and my incessant, negative, chattering thoughts threatened to derail me. Some days, I still hear that familiar refrain, "Who do you think you are?"

I feel a sense of gratitude that before I found running, I'd already been meditating for fifteen years. I also had a solid writing practice, a strong community, several great teachers, mental health medications, and therapy. Movement rounded out that tool kit.

I quickly realized I could meditate while I ran. Infusing the thoughts and body sensations that arise on a run with focused attention and a calm attitude makes running less difficult and more interesting.

Meditative skills keep me going when willpower fails.

In the years since that life-changing social media post, I have run nearly 12,000 miles, including two ultramarathons, three full marathons, thirty-six half marathons in twenty-three states, and more than 100 shorter races.

While those numbers may sound impressive, what counts is my improved inner fitness. I went from a woman who wanted to die to one who thrives. I feel more stable, calm, caring toward others, and interested in the world than before. That inner transformation motivated me to share this practice.

Mindfulness Meditation

Hundreds of definitions exist for the word "meditation." The type of meditation I practice follows a tradition dating back thousands of years: Vipassana, insight, often translated "to see clearly." The technique is called "mindfulness."

Jon Kabat-Zinn, creator of the Stress Reduction Clinic and Center for Mindfulness in Medicine, Health Care, and Society at the University of Massachusetts Medical School offers an elegant definition:

"Mindfulness means paying attention in a particular way, on
purpose, in the present moment, nonjudgmentally, as if your life
depended on it."

—Jon Kabat-Zinn[3]

Rather than escape from experiences, mindfulness meditation teaches us
to be fully present with them. Instead of escaping from our lives, we escape
into them.

I learned to meditate while I was moving, and you can too.

Why this form of meditation and not others?

My experience, the experience of countless others, and scientific studies
confirm[4] that these practices—ones that teach you how to keep your head
where your feet are—offer freedom from suffering.

If you already have a movement form you enjoy, learning to meditate while
you move can refresh, deepen, and renew that movement while opening
new doorways of discovery. If you already meditate regularly, attend
retreats, or even have a teacher, this book can freshen your practice by
adding a new dimension: meditation in motion. If you've fallen away from
any practice, the suggestions in these pages might bring you back to a joy
you once knew.

If you do not have a movement practice, I can help you find one you love and
show you how to infuse that with meditative awareness and a calmness of
mind to create something beyond *exercise*—a practice of transformation.

How does meditation create this transformation?

Meditation teaches you how to be in the present moment. That's the point.

---

3   Jon Kabat-Zinn, *Wherever You Go, There You Are: Mindfulness Meditation in Everyday
    Life*. (New York: Hyperion) 4.

4   Zeis "30 Evidence-Based Benefits of Meditation."

Why the present moment?

The present moment is the only reality, the only thing actually happening. The future has not yet occurred. The past is over. Only in this moment do we have the opportunity to find peace, offer forgiveness, change, and grow. Now is the only moment over which we have any control: right here, right now.

Aren't we right here all the time? What's the difference?

The difference is what you do with your mind.

Let's say you are ice skating. It's crisp, but you're layered. As you glide around the rink, the motion warms your body. This is the perfect opportunity for movement meditation.

As you skate, you notice pleasant body sensations: the sway of your body, the sound of each blade against the ice, the heat generated by your moving limbs. Positive thoughts may also arise: I am graceful, dancing, alive.

You hone your attention on the thoughts and body sensations of skating. Those thoughts and body sensations bring you right into the moment, fully absorbed. Instead of daydreaming or comparing yourself to the skater at the other end of the rink, your meditation skills keep your mind where your body is. You become curious about how it feels to skate, experiencing your body sensations all the way through, learning from what you find. You don't struggle with your mind. You become the motion, opening to it and relaxing around it. While your thoughts may wander to what's for lunch or that big work project, you gently bring your attention back to the present, to your moving body.

All of this is right here. Right now.

A couple of important things are at work here.

First, you'll experience the *mind-body connection* as the separation between your mind and your body begins to disappear.

Second, you'll experience pleasure both from the focus you are developing and from the movements. Because you enjoy these, you continue to meditate and move and feel better physically and emotionally.

Third, that pleasure also helps you overcome any resistance or negativity you may have, at first around movement and eventually around other daily things as well.

Fourth, as the negativity begins to drop away, you'll be less reactive to and gentler with yourself and others. You'll build more equanimity—a curiosity and calm openness of mind, and a non-reactive attitude—allowing you to befriend the thoughts and sensations that arise. These benefits lead to improved mood and energy.

Finally, it can lead to insight into how pushing and pulling on reality causes suffering, not just yours, but everyone else's as well. As you skate or run or dance or jump or pitch or hit or throw, you'll see the habits of mind, heart, and body that cause us all such agony.

The skills and insight gained through practice serve us everywhere for the rest of our lives. Once we taste this wisdom, the world opens. We truly see a child's smile, taste our food, and smell the flowers more than just figuratively. Actions as simple as sensing which foot goes through the door first, feeling your hand grip the racquet, or noticing one breath all the way through can train the mind.

Once you get that, it can change your life in the same positive, helpful way it changed mine.

That's a bold claim.

Yes, and I'm not the only one making it. Let's look at the science.

Benefits of Movement

Before I talk about the benefits of combining movement with meditation, let's look at the well-researched benefits of movement alone.[5] Those of us who already enjoy a movement form already know. We experience them! If you haven't embraced movement (yet) or don't know about the ways movement improves your life, here are some benefits:

Physical

- Lowers blood pressure
- Improves bone health
- Reduces blood sugar
- Enhances weight loss
- Improves cardiovascular health
- Increases breathing and lung capacity
- Manages menopausal symptoms
- Slows the aging process
- Provides pain relief

Cognitive

- Improves reading skill
- Helps grow brain cells
- Enhances learning
- Promotes retention of information

Psychological

- Improves self-esteem
- Helps manage attention and hyperactivity
- Reduces addiction
- Decreases depressive symptoms

---

5   John J. Ratey, *Spark: The Revolutionary New Science of Exercise and the Brain* (New York: Little, Brown, 2018) 79.

- Improves mood and
  mood stability
- Reduces anxiety
- Reduces stress

About stress:

> "At every level from the microcellular to the psychological,
> exercise not only wards off the ill effects of chronic stress; it
> can also reverse them. Studies show that if researchers exercise
> rats that have been chronically stressed, that activity makes
> the hippocampus grow back to its pre-shriveled state. The
> mechanisms by which exercise changes how we think and feel are
> so much more effective than donuts, medicines, and wine. When
> you say you feel less stressed out after you go for a swim, or even
> a fast walk, you are."
>
> —John J. Ratey, author of *Spark: The Revolutionary New Science of
> Exercise and the Brain*[6]

And let's not forget exercising with your family, dog, friends, or a group. Exercise can be a bonding experience too.

Benefits of Meditation

What about meditation? What benefits can we derive from practicing that? In his article "30 Evidence-Based Benefits of Meditation,"[7] meditation instructor and researcher Patrick Zeis set forth a comprehensive list of the physical, mental, and cognitive benefits of meditation and cited studies to support each item. Rather than attempt to recreate his comprehensive research, I'll summarize his points here:

---

6   John J. Ratey, Spark, 79.

7   Patrick Zeis "30 Evidence-Based Benefits of Meditation." www.balancedachievement.
     com/areas-of-life/benefits-of-meditation.

Physical

- Boosts the immune system
- Improves sleep quality & helps treat insomnia
- Lowers blood pressure levels
- Helps treat chronic pain
- Increases energy levels
- Helps alleviate symptoms of premenstrual syndrome
- Slows the body's aging process
- Helps treat migraine headaches
- Improves overall heart health
- Improves management of diabetes

Psychological

- Decreases levels of stress
- Improves emotional intelligence (EI) skills
- Helps combat anxiety
- Helps treat depression
- Relieves symptoms of post-traumatic stress disorder (PTSD)
- Helps treat addiction & reduces relapse rates
- Improves relationships
- Decreases emotional reactivity & increases resiliency
- Improves self-esteem & subjective well-being
- Decreases binge eating & emotional eating

Cognitive

- Improves memory
- Improves executive function processes
- Reduces risk of dementia
- Improves creative thinking skills
- Rebuilds brain's gray matter
- Helps manage symptoms of ADHD

- Increases focus & productivity
- Reduces cognitive rigidity
- Reduces negative rumination
- Promotes positive changes in brainwave frequencies

Even after having meditated for decades, seeing the full list of benefits in black and white happily stunned me.

Benefits of Movement Meditation

Finally, what additional benefits come from combining meditation with movement?

- Some people find movement easier than sitting
- Movement adds interest to meditation
- Movement introduces more things on which to focus during meditation (and vice versa)
- Movement is more concrete and aids with focus
- Movement is novice-friendly
- You don't have to set aside a special time; you're already exercising
- You can do movement meditation anywhere
- Movement meditation may enhance performance

When we meditate while moving, we take meditation *on the road*. It joins the mental world with the physical world, creating a unifying experience that can transfer to every moment and every part of life.

This transferable skill set helps you be present all day long. Once you learn to be mindfully awake during exercise, you will learn to do it when you get a cup of coffee, talk to your boss, watch a movie, and have dinner with your loved ones. Mindfulness *on foot* creates a powerful tool in your life skills toolset. You'll train yourself to be mindful throughout your day.

Neuroplasticity

Scientists originally thought the brain was unchangeable once we reached adulthood. The consensus was that, at some point, growth stopped, and the brain remained static until old age, when brain function regressed. Recent studies show the brain is much more malleable and therefore trainable than previously thought.

Meditators have known this for centuries. But it didn't have a name. The word for this is "neuroplasticity." We can literally rebuild our brains, rewire them, and create new pathways and new habits as a result of this activity. But we can't do it merely by thinking about it. We do it by *action*. One of these actions is meditation.

What is neuroplasticity? It is "the brain's ability to modify, change, and adapt both structure and function throughout life and in response to experience."[8] In short, it's the ability of your brain to change. It can change in response to damage—rebuilding pathways to compensate for areas lost to injury or illness. And it can change in response to learning.

Meditation and movement train the brain. Meditation, the original brain training, is a method of rewiring circuitry based on thousands of years of practice. Recent research shows that movement aids that process.

"Far from being hardwired, as scientists once envisioned it, the brain is constantly being rewired. I'm here to teach you how to be your own electrician."

—John J. Ratey, *Spark: The Revolutionary New Science of Exercise and the Brain*[9]

---

8   Patrice Voss, Maryse E. Thomas, J. Miguel Cisneros-Franco, and Étienne de Villers-Sidani, Department of Neurology and Neurosurgery, Montreal Neurological Institute, McGill University, Montreal, QC, Canada Front. Psychol., October 4, 2017. | doi.org/10.3389/fpsyg.2017.01657.

9   John J. Ratey, *Spark: The Revolutionary New Science of Exercise and the Brain.* www.hachettebookgroup.com/titles/john-j-ratey-md/spark/9781549108297.

Sadly, your brain will also adopt your negative patterns. High amounts of screen time and the instant gratification of social media trains our brains toward inattention. We combat this with activities that train attention in positive ways.

Finally, despite the wonders of neuroplasticity, don't believe the hype. You can't be whoever you want simply by believing hard enough or thinking your way into (or out of) things.

Still, we do what we can, including movement meditation.

Insight

The insights I mentioned earlier might be the best reasons to bother adding meditation to your movement.

When I began to slow jog in middle age, running quickly became my go-to mood lifter. But soon after I'd started to run, a doctor told me I shouldn't because of a congenital defect in my ankle. With his words, my depression began to return.

I was fortunate to have both a meditation practice and a good psychiatrist. The insight gained from meditation ("Um, wait...I'm already running, and my ankle is okay") and my psychiatrist's inquiry (Who is that guy anyway?) gave me the courage to question the doctor and find out for myself if what he said was true. (Spoiler alert: It wasn't.) A decade later, I gratefully continue to use movement meditation as part of my mental health tool kit.

When we meditate, these insights become common. They could be as simple as "Oh! Now, I understand why that piece of the shelf doesn't fit," or as complex as, "Wow! I just experienced a hit of oneness. This is so cool!"

Insights can be about relationships or humanity or your whole purpose for being. Each is as important as the next. Later, I will talk more about what to do with insights, especially the *big* ones that might change your life's direction.

Insight can arise as a thought or a body sensation, such as a deep *knowing* in your gut. These insights, especially ones that change a perspective or inform you, provide another powerful reason to meditate. They differ from thinking about something. It's the same mechanism at work when you get your best ideas in the shower, right before you fall asleep, or when you first wake in the morning. Something pops in. It's a bit of an *aha* moment.

As a writer, I welcome this part of the creative process. I trust that letting go of a problem and heading out for a walk or run might bring a solution my logical mind couldn't find. Of course, there is a time and place to think, analyze, and strategize. But meditation is a time to let all of that go. It offers a technique to encourage those openings, creating conditions that allow insights to happen naturally, in their own time, even while we're moving.

Is This as Powerful as Sitting?

I'm often asked whether it's possible to achieve the same deep mind states, level of focus and concentration, powerful letting go energy, and revelatory insight in mindful movement as in more formal sitting practice.

It depends.

It depends on what you put into it: time, effort, attention, attitude, and willingness—all the things that make up any practice.

And it depends on how much of that letting go energy (equanimity) you develop. Sometimes, even if you do all the right things, nothing you expect or want happens. That's the thing about this practice. As soon as you try too hard to get somewhere, you are lost. Does that mean you won't try? Nope. You will, just as I do. We all need to be reminded. Yes, you learn skills, but ultimately, those skills help you to be right here, as you are, accepting and noticing that. It is human nature to strive. We notice striving and make it part of the practice.

Long retreats often open with several days devoted solely to counting the breath. Some teachers suggest you cannot properly do body or thought-focused meditation without first developing deep focus and concentration. Under this theory, without first building those attention skills, your mind will simply jump from thing to thing, and the retreat would be a waste of time.

Stillness in the body does create an environment for stillness in the mind. The mind moves where the body goes. And it might be true that a still body creates a better atmosphere for the mind to settle. Plus, the historic Buddha found enlightenment *sitting* under the Bodhi tree, rather than dancing beneath it or running laps around it.

Does that make sitting better than movement meditation?

Not exactly. They are simply different. It's like comparing typing to writing by hand. You might have a preference, and different parts of the brain light up when you write by hand rather than type, but the result is the same: words on a page. You might even switch from one to another, the way a tennis player might also lift weights. But the final product is a book or an article or a poem (or a workout). I doubt the tai chi master or experienced yoga instructor would say their form is better than any other. That's not the way Eastern philosophy works.

Beyond this question of which is more valuable, let's consider a practical question: *Which meditation practice will you actually do?*

If sitting practice does not appeal to you and movement does, voilà! It's much better to do any practice at all than to choose a supposedly superior practice and not do it.

Don't tangle yourself up over this. Consult a teacher, a mentor, or a book, and check yourself. See if you're faking or half-assing meditation, while remembering that any meditation is better than none at all. Leave perfectionism at the door, or use it as your object of meditation! Just meditate, and don't worry about whether you're getting anywhere (unless you and your dog are six miles out and need to get back to your car). Just choose *something*. Be with that. And do your best to let go of any need to find the correct or perfect way.

Finally, why not both sit and move?

The path has many doors. Enter through any. Sit one day. Walk the next. Dance the next. The options are infinite. It may benefit you to focus on one *posture* (one movement form), but if that choice means you don't meditate at all, mix it up. The best meditation is the one you do.

Summary

Research supports numerous physical, psychological, and cognitive benefits of both movement and meditation. Who doesn't want more brain cells? And my anecdotal research shows that combining the two adds even more benefits.

Mindfulness meditation is:

- Infusing present-moment experience (thoughts and body sensations) with equanimity (a composed mind state even in the face of difficulty).
- A set of learned skills that will help you accept reality, exactly as it is at any moment.
- Being here now.

I see that turning my movement into a meditation might have some merit, but how the heck do you do it?

Turn the page, and I'll show you.

CHAPTER 2

HOW TO MEDITATE
WHILE YOU MOVE

Shinzen's Answer
to Everything

If you asked venerable meditation teacher and Vajrayana monk Shinzen
Young how to meditate while you move, he would suggest you "Infuse your
experience with awareness and equanimity."[10] At least, that was the answer
he gave no matter what question he was asked at the numerous retreats Ed
and I attended, as well as in talks on the more than one hundred cassette
tapes to which we listened.

It didn't matter if the person wanted to know how to work with joy,
boredom, ecstasy, anger, glee, agony, titillation, jealousy, jubilation, pain
(physical or emotional), happiness, grief, greed, resentment, sadness,
splendor, or terror; Shinzen gave the same answer. His instruction is the
essence of mindfulness meditation. I'm not one for tattoos, but if I were, I'd
have that inked on my arm.

---

10   Shinzen Young, "Dharma Talk," (retreat lecture, Northridge, CA, January 18, 1994).

> "Infuse your experience with awareness and equanimity."
>
> —Shinzen Young[11]

Let's break it down:

Experience

Your "experience" is your thoughts and body sensations—including your breath—happening in real time, right now, where you are standing, lying down, sitting, or, for our purposes, moving. In mindfulness meditation, you choose an aspect of your experience (your thoughts and body sensations) on which to focus.

Infuse

"Infuse" in this context is how you direct your awareness, the energy of concentration with which you place your attention on your "experience."

Awareness

"Awareness," often called "attention," is the quality of how you direct your mind. This Zen story explains how essential attention is:

11 Shinzen Young, "Dharma Talk."

"A student said to Master Ichu, 'Please write for me something of great wisdom.' Master Ichu picked up his brush and wrote one word: 'Attention.' The student said, 'Is that all?' The master wrote, 'Attention. Attention.' The student became irritable. 'That doesn't seem profound or subtle to me.' In response, Master Ichu wrote simply, 'Attention. Attention. Attention.' In frustration, the student demanded, 'What does this word 'attention' mean?' Master Ichu replied, 'Attention means attention.' "

—Charlotte Joko Beck[12]

When you begin to meditate, you build a focused, concentrated attention. It's a muscle that meditation strengthens.

Equanimity

Finally, and possibly most important, let's define "equanimity." This mind state is the ability to not struggle with whatever experience you have during your practice. Shinzen calls it "not fighting with yourself."

Merriam Webster defines equanimity as "evenness of mind, especially under stress"[13] while Dictionary.com defines it as "mental calmness, especially in a difficult situation."[14]

In their online course, "Dhamma Wheel," *Tricycle Magazine* calls equanimity "the secret ingredient of mindfulness, indeed of the entire Buddhist approach to practice."[15] They explain:

---

12   Joko Beck, "Attention Means Attention," Tricycle Magazine, Fall 1993. tricycle.org/magazine/attention-means-attention.

13   "Equanimity." Merriam-Webster.com. 2021. www.merriam-webster.com/dictionary/equanimity (November 11, 2021).

14   "Equanimity." Dictionary.com. 2021. www.dictionary.com/browse/equanimity (November 11, 2021).

15   Dhamma Wheel Online Course - Right Intention: Developing Equanimity, November 23, 2021. learn.tricycle.org/p/dhamma-wheel.

"Like the clutch of a car, which disengages the engine from the wheels, freeing them to revolve independently, equanimity disengages us from the compulsion of the pleasure/pain reflex, freeing us to experience a range of sensations without craving."[16]

—Dhamma Wheel, Tricycle Magazine

To develop equanimity, Dhamma Wheel recommends:

"...bringing an attitude of 'this is simply what is happening now' toward whatever occurs, instead of 'I like [or don't like] this,' or 'I approve [or don't approve] of this.' "[17]

—Dhamma Wheel, Tricycle Magazine

Here's another definition:

"In the deepest forms of insight, we see that things change so quickly that we can't hold onto anything, and eventually the mind lets go of clinging. Letting go brings equanimity; the greater the letting go, the deeper the equanimity."[18]

—Vipassana Master Sayadaw U Pandita

If we expand Shinzen's suggestion to include these definitions, it becomes:

- Infuse (focus on)
- Your experience (thoughts and body sensations)
- With awareness (concentration)
- And equanimity (a balanced mind).

---

16   Dhamma Wheel Online Course - Right Intention: Developing Equanimity, November 23, 2021. learn.tricycle.org/p/dhamma-wheel.

17   Dhamma Wheel Online Course - Right Intention: Developing Equanimity, December 21, 2021. learn.tricycle.org/p/dhamma-wheel.

18   "A Perfect Balance: Cultivating Equanimity" with Gil Fronsdal and Sayadaw U Pandita, *Tricycle*, Winter 2005. tricycle.org/magazine/perfect-balance.

Steps to Make Any Move a Meditation

To put Shinzen's answer in motion and make any movement a meditation, follow these steps:

1.   Choose a form of movement.

2.   Choose an interval or period of time.

3.   Choose an aspect of experience (i.e., an object of meditation).

4.   Begin the movement practice. As you move, place your awareness on the object you have chosen.

5.   When your mind wanders, gently bring your attention back to your chosen object of meditation.

6.   Do all of this gently, with no strain and no self-judgment. Be curious and open, interested and aware.

7.   If your body and/or mind respond, acknowledge that response, then either return to your original object of meditation or intentionally make the response your new object of meditation.

8.   If you forget how to implement this, contact a qualified teacher who will help you remember.

Here's an example of how I do it:

1.   *Movement form*: running. Big surprise.

2.   *Interval*: the first mile.

3.   *Object (experience)*: the sensations in my left foot.

4.   *Place awareness on the object*: I start to run and direct my attention toward my left foot, letting my focus sink into the sensations as they exist in real time. I'm not thinking about my foot or imagining my foot. I'm attending to what my foot really feels like.

5. *Mind wanders, gently bring it back*: I begin to daydream about breakfast. I remember I decided to meditate. I gently return my attention to that left foot.

6. *Recycle any reaction*: If I feel irritated at not being able to daydream about breakfast, I give that part of myself a little nod and remind it we'll get to eat breakfast in real life, later. I return to my left foot.

7. *Gentle*: As I continue to run and meditate, I notice any physical strain, mental judgment, or emotional tussles. I do my best to be with those while returning the attention to my left foot.

8. *Ask for help*: If I have difficulty (physical or emotional) or am confused, or if anything too upsetting arises, I contact a meditation teacher, a medical professional, or a therapist.

Let's look at each of these steps more closely.

One: Choose a Movement Form

The first step in making movement a meditation is choosing a form of movement.

I already have a movement form. Do I need a different one?

If you already enjoy a particular form of movement, feel free to use that for your movement meditation practice. If you don't already have a movement practice or have other questions about this step, head to the chapter on "More About Forms of Movement." Otherwise, work with the form you have.

Two: Choose an Interval

The second step in making movement a meditation is choosing an interval. Often this is a period of time.

Choosing an interval creates a structure, a container for the meditation practice. In sitting meditation, the leader rings a bell to open the period of meditation and rings the bell again to close it. That's the container: bell to bell.

Choosing an interval also gives your practice a boost by creating a tiny pressure cooker effect. This heightens awareness and raises the stakes a little. Remind your mind, "I can do anything for five minutes."

I say "interval" as opposed to "time period" because you don't have to measure it in minutes. It can be time or distance or a particular part of your workout.

It can be:

- From this driveway to that driveway.
- Every chorus of this song (if music is part of the practice).
- Only when I'm serving.
- When I'm at the foul line.
- Just during the tee-offs.
- Only the Wednesday hill repeats, and only the downhills.

Be very specific with this. The mind likes to wriggle around. Being specific helps it calm.

Three: Choose an Object of Meditation

The third step in making movement a meditation is choosing an object of meditation. This is the "experience" Shinzen suggests infusing with awareness and equanimity. It's the place in the present moment where you settle the mind during a particular meditation session. This can be a specific part or function of your body, including your breath or your thoughts.

You choose the object of meditation, unless a teacher is guiding you or you are listening to a guided meditation. You set the intention.

Objects of meditation fall into two broad categories: *thoughts* and *body sensations*. The breath is a body sensation. Any thoughts that arise about your breathing are, obviously, thoughts.

Body sensations and thoughts occur in real time. When you focus your mind on any one of those, it naturally draws the mind into the now, anchoring you in the present.

What about emotions? Can I choose those?

Yes. But in doing so, you're still choosing to focus on thoughts and body sensations. We usually aren't aware of it, but any emotional state— resistance, encouragement, joy, or bliss—is a blend of thoughts and body sensations. Meditation helps untangle those. (See Chapter 7: "Tangles of Emotion.")

I thought I wasn't supposed to think!

You can't not think. But meditation practice creates conditions that allow your thoughts to slow or even stop. This will not happen by force. None of this is about force. You take the action, and the process works on you. The only *force* is the intention to try this type of practice and possibly the will it takes to put on your running shoes, your dance leotard, or your tennis shorts. Otherwise, you allow the process to happen. That's equanimity.

Four: Place Your Awareness on the Object of Meditation

Once you have chosen your object of meditation, the fourth step of making any movement a meditation is placing your attention on that object and allowing your awareness to sink in.

Think of your attention like the lens of a camera. Once your concentration grows, you'll be able to zone in on one spot and go deep—piercing that object of meditation intensely with a very close view—or you can widen your awareness. You can open it slightly wider, all the way, or anything in between. For now, until you develop that concentration, choose one object and stay with it through the interval of practice. Once you build that focus, try other methods. Concentration has many benefits, including adding more pleasure to the movement you already enjoy.

I frequently have sensations in my left foot. They call to me. I notice pulses and shifts, warmth and coolness. They are neutral but present, making it easy to direct my attention toward them. As you become familiar with this practice, you may find something similar in your body calling to you. Use that.

Direct Your Attention

YOUR TURN: DIRECT YOUR ATTENTION

Point your mind to your left foot. Don't look at it with your eyes: "Feel it" with your mind. An image of your foot or shoe might arise. Let that drop. Instead, feel what your foot feels like. Is it warm or cold? Does it tingle? Is it still? Moving? Are these sensations pleasant, unpleasant, or neutral? If you have trouble, wiggle your toes just enough to get in touch with the sensations. Otherwise, don't move your foot. Simply be with it exactly as it is. For those moments when you are feeling your left foot, those left foot sensations are your object of meditation.

Noting and Labeling

You can also note and label as you meditate. Noting and labeling can help the mind settle and regain focus if thoughts become intrusive. It's another way to develop concentration and increase focus and attention.

"Note" a thought or sensation by intentionally acknowledging it as you experience it. Then, if you choose, give it a label by either speaking aloud or mentally saying a word "label."

When you note and label, you are not thinking. Rather, you observe and thumbtack the experience with a single, neutral word. Speak the label aloud to yourself, or say it under your breath in real time as sensations occur.

Here are some examples:

- Walking: "lift, shift, place."
- Running: "left, left, left."
- Weight lifting: "lift, up, pull."
- Dance: "place, lift, twirl."

Use a word label to describe a sensation, like "hot," "pulsing," or "throbbing." Be aware of any judgment that arises with the description. Don't add a color as a descriptor unless you physically see that color, not if you just imagine it. If you do see a color, label it as "green," "blue," "yellow," etc. Only note and label what you experience, not what you imagine.

Take care not to get too caught up in labeling, especially if your movement requires a series of quick movements. A speed skater won't be able to label each move.

Gauge the intensity of your concentration by how frequently you label. If the labels are quick, your mind might be jumping around. Use noting and labels to help your consciousness sink into the object of meditation. Start by labeling during a slower movement. During quick movement, you might not need to label so long as you can maintain your concentration.

Also, notice if labeling leads you into thinking. Are you more aware of the moment? If so, the labels are effective. Labeling should lead you into the moment, not away from it.

If you begin to worry whether you are noting and labeling properly, note that!

YOUR TURN: NOTING AND LABELING

Take a walk. As you walk, direct your attention to whatever body part is most prominent. Let's say it's your left foot. As you walk, keep your attention on the sensations of that foot. When your mind wanders, gently bring it back to the feeling of that foot, but add a label: foot. Each time your left foot hits the ground, either silently or quietly say "foot." Continue for whatever interval of time you like.

Counting

Another way to keep your mind on the object of meditation you've chosen is to try a counting exercise. Counting is a basic form of noting. It builds concentration and calms the mind by giving it a little task.

Counting works best with repetitive movement. Count steps while walking or running, arm strokes while swimming, swings while practicing any racquet sport.

You can also count your breath. Do this by counting from one to ten. On the inhale, count "one." On the exhale, count "two," and "three" on the next inhale. When you reach ten, either count backward from nine down to one, or start at one again. Any time you lose count or thoughts distract you, begin again at one.

Be creative. Count breaths or steps as you carry your bag from the tee to your next shot. If it's in the rough or the sand, you'll need that concentration. Count steps or breaths as you walk to the basketball foul line, training yourself in focus and patience. Count repetitions or foot falls. Any counting will build concentration, and in all likelihood, patience too.

Don't be discouraged if you don't make it to ten with anything you count. As with any other new endeavor, this will get easier as you build your meditation skills of concentration and calm.

YOUR TURN: COUNTING

Go for another walk. As you move, place your attention somewhere on your right arm. Each time your right arm swings forward, count: one, two, three, etc., up to ten. When you get to ten, begin again at one. If your mind wanders, gently bring it back to the real-time sensations of your right arm and begin to count at one again. Continue for whatever interval of time you like.

Five: When Your Mind Wanders, Gently Bring It Back

By now, as you attempt to meditate while you move, you have probably experienced your mind wandering. The fifth step in making movement a meditation, a vital step, is gently bringing your mind back to your object of meditation. In doing so, you build that calmness of mind: equanimity.

Your mind will naturally wander. The mind's job is to think thoughts. Dealing with a wandering mind is simple, but not always easy. When your thinking strays, first notice that you remembered you were meditating. Maybe even give yourself a mental cheer for that. Whole meditation sessions can pass without such remembering. Then, once you have remembered, gently return your attention to your selected object of meditation.

Think of an analog radio dial, a round knob turned to tune the radio to a station. You might catch a frequency between stations. The signal isn't clear. You turn the dial until it is.

Recently, Scarlet (a.k.a., "the pupperina"), a yellow Labrador we got after my beloved Morgan died in his old age, and I headed down to the ravine to slow jog a few miles along the pavement. I chose my good friend "left foot" as my object of meditation.

When I felt those wandering-mind sensations, I tuned my awareness to that left foot station. I tuned the dial of attention into that feeling and allowed my consciousness to sink in; this was not forced. I directed my mind, but I did it with focus and concentration, tuning out anything not left foot. I did not imagine my left foot. If I saw an image in my mind, I let that drop. I only attended to the *felt sense* entering through my foot.

Despite years of practice, thousands of miles of running, and a strong attempt to focus, thoughts intruded: *What are you trying to prove? You're old, fat, and slow!* On and on they droned. *You'll never be a real runner.*

Then I remembered. I was meditating! I had selected left foot sensations as my object.

This moment and what I did with it was the most important part of this and any meditation session.

I gave myself a tiny pat on the back for remembering, then gently, gently, gently brought my mind back to the real-time sensations in my left foot.

It would have been easy to heap more chiding and berating thoughts on top of the negative voices already at work, but I did not.

With practice, I have learned never to yell at myself or reprimand myself for being distracted.

And I would be this gentle no matter the nature of the distraction.

When your mind wanders, pay attention to two things:

First: remembering.

Ah! I was meditating. Ah! I forgot. Ah! I was distracted. Give yourself a little mental pat on the back for noticing. The mind often hops from left foot to bluebird to our neighbor singing to the dog panting to our grocery list to the local news scene to the fate of the nation to the futility of existence without remembering we were meditating. Some days, that will be the full experience. Give yourself credit when you remember. That's tremendous.

Second: gentleness.

Notice the tone you take with yourself when you remember. Is it harsh or callous? Are you yelling? Be aware of that. Don't try to change it. Become awake to the fact that this is how you treat yourself. Let any feeling state that arises from that tone become part of your practice. Open to that harshness. Do your best to let it transform on its own, into compassion for yourself. It is enough to notice when that mind state arises. Attention to it will "love" it into change.

The most apt metaphor, especially appropriate for a dog-lover like me, is to think of your mind like a puppy you are trying to train to walk on a leash. The puppy has no idea what you want. It wants to please, but it also wants to play. It does not yet know the joy of making you happy. How would you treat this puppy? Would you yell at it or kick it or yank the leash so hard it was lifted off its little paws? Only a monster would do that, or someone with a temper too short to be trusted with a puppy.

Sadly, that's how many people treat their minds. They punish the puppy, or they give up, saying the puppy is not trainable. They don't have the patience.

The owner who loves the puppy into behavior takes the gentle approach. She coaxes the puppy with gentle nudges. She reminds the puppy of the way to go. She might redirect and tug on the leash to get the puppy's attention.

But she will use positive reinforcement, lots of "atta-girl" and "way to go" cheering on every little step. This is how I trained first Morgan and later Scarlet to run at my side: gentle nudges with lots of praise.

Work with this attitude. It will take time.

You are learning skills few do. You are teaching your baby puppy mind something new. At first, your mind will not understand the benefit of what you are trying to teach it. It may resist. It may throw a little tantrum. It may tell you to quit or try to convince you this is a waste of time. I promise you it is not. You will find benefit, but only if you give it a chance.

YOUR TURN: BRING YOUR MIND BACK

How about another walk? As you move, notice your breath. Find the place in your chest or belly where the sensation of breathing is most readily apparent. Place your attention there. Let your awareness sink into that as your object of meditation. Continue to attend to the breath until your mind wanders. When you realize your mind has wandered, give yourself a little mental pat on the back for remembering. Then, with equanimity, gently bring your attention back to the sensation of your breath. If you find any part of this difficult, thank your mind for those thoughts, and again, gently redirect your focus back to your breath. Continue for whatever interval of time you like.

Six: Be Gentle with Yourself

The sixth step of making any move a meditation isn't actually a step at all. It's a state of mind called equanimity, a crucial part of "Shinzen's Answer to Everything" and an element essential to meditation practice. In the previous steps and exercises, I used the word "gently" and talked about training the puppy mind. Equanimity is so fundamental to making any move a meditation that I don't apologize for the repetition.

Our experiences (thoughts and body sensations) do a little dance, then pass away in a process called impermanence. Equanimity not only allows this to happen, but it helps us see it in real time. By not pushing or pulling on our inner experience, we can be fully present for our outer experiences, including our movement practice.

One way to develop equanimity is through curiosity. When I'm walking the pupperina and I start to think about politics and judgment arises in response, I note those feelings, but I also try to get curious about it. Can I open to it instead of tightening? Is another sensation under the unpleasantness? Can I relax around it? Even if it feels like a rock in my gut or bricks on my shoulders, there is usually space somewhere. I note that, too. This process is equanimity.

YOUR TURN: EQUANIMITY

You guessed it: Take a walk. They're good for you! Use the breath as your focus again. When you find the place in your belly or chest where each breath is most apparent, take a few minutes as you walk to let your mind settle there. Let the natural rhythm of the breath calm you. Once you're focused there, note other thoughts and sensations arising. Is there pleasure in the breath and the motion of walking? Or do you feel resistance? Are you bored? Whatever comes up, do your best to acknowledge it. Allow it to well up and pass away. Wandering thoughts or your inability to see this might frustrate you. Acknowledge that as well. Continue for whatever interval of time you like.

Seven: Recycle Any Reaction

The seventh step of making any move a meditation is what Shinzen calls, "Recycle the reaction." Anything that arises during practice offers yet another opportunity for practice—grist for the mill and all that.

One day in Zumba, you've chosen the tips of the fingers of your right hand as your object of meditation because sensations there come naturally. Then the second song comes on, and you hate it. You feel your neck tense and a frown form. You think "Why this song today of all days?" You acknowledge the thoughts and frustrated feelings, then turn your attention back to your fingers. This works for the rest of that song, but you dislike the third song even more than the one before. Your frustration grows. Here's where that choice I mentioned comes in.

Although you originally set an intention to meditate on your fingertips, you can choose, with purpose, to set a new intention and focus your awareness on the sensations of frustration, making that your new object of meditation. You have now "recycled the reaction."

YOUR TURN: RECYCLE THE REACTION

Time for another walk. If you walk in your sport, do this then. This time, you choose the object of meditation. Pick any body sensation and start moving. When your mind wanders, note the thought, cheer yourself for remembering, then gently and with great equanimity, direct your attention back to your object of meditation. As you walk, be aware of any other sensations. Often, multiple sensations happen at the same time. You might experience the shift of your weight as you move while you also sense the touch of cool air against your cheek.

To build focus, I've directed you to attend to one sensation at a time. When you experience another sensation, make that choice.

Will you stay with the object of meditation you originally chose or set a new intention and redirect your awareness? Since the choice is made consciously, either choice is appropriate. And if you find any part of this difficult, that can become your object of meditation too! Continue for whatever interval of time you like.

Eight: Ask for Help

The final step in this process is bit of a cautionary note, which I will also discuss more later. The eighth step is asking for help when you need it.

This principle, like many things in this book, applies to movement, meditation, and life. Aches and pains? See a trainer. Injured? Visit a physical therapist. Sick? Call your doctor. I'll talk more in detail about teachers and therapists later, but know that a trained meditation professional can often answer your questions if you feel confused or distressed.

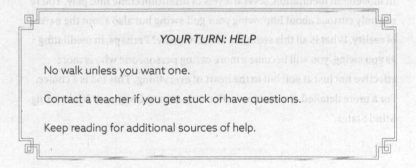

YOUR TURN: HELP

No walk unless you want one.

Contact a teacher if you get stuck or have questions.

Keep reading for additional sources of help.

Intention

Notice the word "choice" in many of the steps. When you choose your movement form, interval, and object of meditation, you have set an intention. I could have called intention "Step Zero" because it influences the other choices and your mindset as you start to practice.

For each session, you choose parameters. They become your aim, setting the tone for that interval. You're not claiming them or visualizing an outcome. You're not creating a checklist of things to accomplish. It's more like selecting a type of workout. Will you practice your serve or your return? Will it be speed work or long, slow miles? You intend to do it, and you'll see how it goes.

Generally, meditation intentions are large and universal, beyond any individual goal. They help us see how we are connected to the rest of the world and how each of our thoughts and actions have consequences. Ask yourself what's important to you. What do you value? You might set an intention to see ways to be more effective in your community or the world at large. But an intention can also be personal, such as intending to adopt more gentleness toward yourself and compassion for your family or coworkers. Or it could be as simple as not throwing up during football mat workouts.

In movement meditation, several levels of intention come into play. You're not only curious about improving your golf swing but also about the nature of reality. What is all this swinging about anyway? Perhaps, in meditating as you swing, you will become a more caring person, one who is more effective not just at golf but in the heart of everything. This too is a choice. For a more detailed discussion of intention, turn to Chapter 9: "Cultivating Mind States."

YOUR TURN: INTENTION

The next time you engage in your preferred movement form, follow each of the steps. But first, set an intention, individual and universal. Aim for kindness, graciousness, and peace—as well as your version of hitting them straight and long.

How Often?

How often should I do this practice and for how long?

A Zen master said, "I try to meditate thirty minutes every day, but on tough days, I meditate for an hour." Runners have a similar version. "If running is hard, run more." I'll bet every sport has its own.

The question isn't quantity. You could do your movement meditation practice all day every day, but if you're not focused on what you're doing and applying the technique, you might as well play computer Solitaire. Although, given the right focus and mind state, even computer Solitaire can be a meditation.

Do whatever your sport requires for you to be good enough for you to enjoy it. Any effort, when made with intention, counts. Do it until you want to do it more!

Just watch the trap of creating a story about not doing enough. Stay with the direct sensations or observe the thoughts and let them pass. Please take my word for this. That extra layer of an "I'm not enough" story leads to unnecessary suffering. If those thoughts arise, you and I both need to acknowledge them and let them float on by. Also notice, "This meditation would be better if..." No change needed. Simply be aware. We're doing our best.

Safety First

I slammed hard into the bright white wall of the tai chi studio. A few years before I began to run, I took the Nia Technique white belt training. During one day of the course, our teacher instructed each of us trainees to free dance, moving spontaneously. When my turn came, I concentrated hard, allowing my body to move as it wanted, deeply focused on thoughts and body sensations. And I didn't see the wall coming. Gratefully, I bounced onto the floor with no injury. But it taught me a strong lesson: Safety first.

Sitting meditation rarely poses any physical threat. Although you could conceivably sprain a wrist if you fall asleep and slide onto the floor while meditating in a chair, meditation generally offers a safe way to practice something powerful and sublime.

But when you combine meditation practice with movement and that movement happens outdoors, and especially if that outdoors includes motorized vehicles such as the cars in your neighborhood or barnyard animals (think yoga with goats), the chances of injury increase exponentially.

Stay aware of your surroundings. Be mindful not just of your object of meditation, but of the things happening at the edges of your awareness. Those baby goats you're frolicking with in downward dog have sharp little hooves.

Be practical.

If you're running or walking on a street, face traffic. If you're outdoors at night anywhere near vehicles, wear a lighted vest or, at minimum, a reflector. Inexpensive, clip-on blinkers might mean the difference between you coming home safely and your loved ones receiving a heartbreaking call.

Who Is This Practice For?

Who should undertake this training?

The great thing about mindful movement is that there's no minimum requirement, no prerequisite, and no basic fitness level required. It also doesn't matter if you have never meditated or never even heard of meditation. Anyone who has access to this information—regardless of socioeconomic class, race, religion (or lack thereof), gender, education level, and size or shape—can meditate.

But formal meditation practice is more readily available to middle- and upper-class people who can afford to take time off from work and family to attend retreats and spend time with teachers. The same is true of movement. Racism, poverty, mobility issues, and other factors may limit someone's ability to study or move the way they wish, or at all.

That's part of why I wrote this book: to make movement and meditation accessible. Don't have time to sit? No worries. Meditate while you take care of your family, while you work, while you commute. Meditate on the go. I want everyone interested to enjoy the benefits of movement meditation. No one should be denied the ability to be free from suffering.

So, start exactly where you are. It's perfectly grand to be your current shape, size, and fitness level. It's tremendous to be at whatever stage in meditation practice you are, from beginner to experienced. And wherever you are on the mental health and wellness continuum is fine. If you are alive, you are eligible. If you are alive, you have the "equipment" you need. If you are alive, you are ready!

Summary

How do you meditate while you move? Infuse the thoughts and body sensations (your experience) of movement with awareness (focus and concentration) and equanimity (a calm, curious mind).

Here's a recap:

0. Set an intention.

1. Choose a form of movement.

2. Choose an interval or period of time.

3. Choose an aspect of experience (i.e., an object of meditation).

4. Begin the movement practice. As you move, place your awareness on the object you have chosen.

5. When your mind wanders, gently bring your attention back to your chosen object of meditation.

6. Do all of this gently, with no strain and no self-judgment. Be curious and open, interested and aware.

7. If your body and/or mind responds, acknowledge that response and either return to your original object of meditation or intentionally make that response your new object of meditation.

8. If you forget this, contact a qualified teacher who will help you remember.

Bookmark this page. Make a copy and tape it to your mirror. Maybe tattoo this on your arm as well.

Next, I'll share my meditation journey and explain why I stay on this path.

CHAPTER 3

WHY I BOTHER

Why did you first begin to meditate?

There was this guy.

On one of our early dates, he asked, "Wanna sit?" I shrugged. He set the microwave timer for five minutes and said, "Close your eyes. Notice your breath. Try not to fidget."

I did as he instructed, peeking at the microwave clock every few seconds. Five minutes felt like an hour. My mind raced. My breath disappeared. I fidgeted.

While I continued to "sit" with him on a regular basis (I really liked him), I didn't like to meditate. It felt weird, boring, and a little scary. It seemed like a waste of time. And it was sometimes uncomfortable. I wasn't big on discomfort.

A few months later, I reached down to dry my feet after showering and my back went out. My back had been "going out" for years. I was in elementary school when I saw my first chiropractor. Untreated scoliosis, falling off horses, bad posture, and poor core stability made me the perfect candidate for back surgery. I wanted to avoid that.

I strengthened my core, aligned my spine, and tried to keep my back from going out, but the issue continued to flare, especially when I was under stress. And when you're the only woman lawyer in a consulting firm, then become the only woman partner in a small law firm, and you hate conflict on top of it all, stress is unavoidable.

The next time my back went out, that guy I'd been dating (Ed, now my husband of nearly thirty years) handed me a set of Mindfulness Based Stress Reduction (MBSR) cassettes by Jon Kabat-Zinn.

I'd already spent days on the sofa. Time for a new plan. The MBSR postures seemed odd, not quite yoga, not quite physical therapy. Plus, MBSR introduced using mindfulness while moving, essentially meditation in motion.

About the same time, I discovered the Egoscue Method, created by former Marine Corps major and anatomical physiologist Pete Egoscue. After returning from Vietnam in extreme pain, Egoscue designed a course of gentle exercises which encourage the body to return to natural, balanced, postural alignment. The moments I spent lying with my back flat on the floor, legs folded in a ninety-degree angle over the edge of a chair, slowly raising and lowering my arms, offered another opportunity for mindfulness in motion.

Ed also introduced me to the work of Dr. John Sarno, author of *Mind Over Back Pain*. Sarno theorizes that stress, rather than physical injury, causes most back pain. Two people can present with identical injuries and one might have pain and the other not. Sarno proposed making an inquiry regarding subconscious negative emotions and a technique to bring them to awareness. Determined to heal my back without surgery, I willingly tried all these tactics.

Later, through a friend of Ed's, I discovered the work of Shinzen Young. His "Break Through Pain" recordings reinforced what I had learned from Dr. Sarno and Jon Kabat-Zinn. He put it in a centuries-old context. I was already meditating; I just hadn't thought of it that way. Jon Kabat-Zinn probably called it meditation, and I was "sitting" with Ed, but I didn't accept that meditation was actually "doing" anything until I felt the relief myself.

I hadn't realized how much of a story, an unnecessary layer of suffering, I had added on top of the genuine physical pain. Practice revealed my ruminations: "How long will this go on?" and "Will I be paralyzed?" and "Ed must be so tired of hearing me complain. Surely he'll leave." As I learned to let those go, that left only the uncomfortable but tolerable body sensations.

This combination of mindfulness practice, Egoscue, MBSR, and Sarno's inquiry into my emotions worked. My back still spasms at times, especially if I stop doing any of these, but I'm forever grateful to Ed for introducing me to meditation and the other tools which ended the suffering my back pain caused me.

I'm also grateful to that original back pain: It led me to movement meditation. And later I would discover how movement and meditation help with emotional pain as well.

Foundations

Many sources inform my practice. Jacqueline Mandell (now Lama, Honorific Teacher) led the first weekend silent mindfulness retreat I attended at Grailville, in Cincinnati, Ohio, introducing me to formal retreat practice. I attended many retreats she led. About the same time, I picked up Bhante G.'s book, *Mindfulness in Plain English*. It gives simple instruction on mindfulness meditation practice. Reading that helped me make sense of what I was learning, and when I was introduced to Shinzen Young, it became even more clear.

Ed and I attended retreats offered by the Yellow Springs Dharma Center, where I studied with Marcia Rose and other teachers. Since there wasn't a mindfulness group in central Ohio, with the help of several others, Ed and

I began Mindfulness Meditation of Columbus, coordinating retreats with teachers including Bhante G., Lama Mandell, and others.

I also began to study writing practice, a Zen-influenced *writing-as-meditation* technique founded by bestselling author Natalie Goldberg, a student of Zen Master Katagiri Roshi. Natalie invited me to lead meditation at her retreats and writing practice for a private group at her zendo. I have taught writing practice, including sitting and walking meditation, for more than twenty years.

When, after two decades of meditation and writing practice, I began to run, I discovered Katherine and Danny Dreyer's book *ChiRunning* on a library end cap display. I took a ChiRunning workshop from local instructor Doug Dapo, and another piece of my practice "tool kit" came together. ChiRunning helped me refine my understanding of movement meditation.

Although mindful movement meditation is not my only practice, it might be where I learn the most. More importantly, it's the meditation I'm most likely to do!

During the pandemic, I took the meditation leader training with Sage Institute for Creativity and Consciousness led by Sean Tetsudo Murphy, Sensei and received certification.

I add to these conversations a mental health thread. Having lived with depression and anxiety from bipolar disorder for much of my life, well-being has to be in the mix. If I don't attend to those symptoms, I cannot appreciate running. I cannot write well. I cannot be in a functional relationship with Ed, our dog, my family, my friends, or my community. I cannot serve myself or others. Unless I manage my mental health symptoms, I won't be here at all.

The Real Reason I Bother

This is all lovely, but, really, why do you care so much?

Because my attempts to create my reality, fake positive thinking, and be something I wasn't nearly killed me.

For nearly ten years I practiced law. I mostly excelled. I love research and writing. I loved hunting down cases no one else could find. I had great coworkers and liked to dress the part. Unfortunately, I didn't thrive in that high-stress environment. Neither a labor relations consulting firm nor an employment law firm suited my intuitive, peace-loving, daydreamer personality.

But I didn't know that then.

I felt ashamed that I couldn't keep up the fast pace and especially that I did not enjoy conflict. But I sure tried. When I couldn't shape-shift through it, I turned to "positive thinking," "manifest your dreams," and "create your own reality" books and audio recordings.

I continued to deliver the work, but at a huge emotional cost.

Eventually, a day came when pretending failed. Too depressed to complete a project, I failed one of my favorite clients and my partners. I had shape-shifted myself into a mental health nightmare.

But I was also learning to meditate. Soon, I saw the differences in the systems.

Meditation invited me to be present with the pain, fear, anxiety, and conflict—paradoxically, as a way to move beyond the suffering it engendered. It grew harder and harder for me to hide from the reality that I was not only in the wrong job, but possibly the wrong profession.

The "create your reality" message told me I could have whatever I thought I wanted if I just made my mind work for me. When I couldn't make that work, I thought I was doing it wrong. That system told me to envision success, set my fears aside, think positive, align with abundance, and "just do it." But "fake it 'til you make it" only goes so far.

As I tried to manifest a different reality and failed to accept the actual reality—that I needed professional help for long-standing mental health issues and probably a different career—I came close to ending my own life. I thought I needed to kill myself because I wasn't able to manifest my way into practicing law with comfort and ease.

After I got out of the mental health hospital—they saved my life—a psychologist said that me practicing law was the worst case of poor job fit she had seen in more than twenty years of practice. When I explained my attempts to think my way to success or meditate through a breakdown without help, she shook her head. She had heard it from others. An avocado can't think its way into becoming a T-bone steak.

I also thought I had failed at meditation!

Still confused, I called Shinzen. I felt like a failure not only for being unable to practice law, but for needing medication. It seems ridiculous now, but I asked if taking mental health medications made me a lousy meditator!

First, Shinzen wisely reminded me that he is a monk, not a psychiatrist. Once I reassured him that I had mental health professionals, he shared about meditators he knew who needed medication for mental health disorders. "Mindfulness can't fix everything," he said. "But it can reduce the suffering." He reminded me that I had only been meditating a few years. A major depressive episode would challenge even a seasoned meditator.

He encouraged me to continue to practice and suggested I use the thoughts and body sensations of depression as objects of meditation.

Most importantly, Shinzen affirmed that if I needed medication to stay alive, I needed medication—period. That's all it meant. Nothing more. He suggested I let my thoughts around that become part of my practice too.

After the call, my mental health gallows humor kicked in. "Nita. You can't meditate if you're dead."

More than thirty years later, I still twitch when someone says "manifest positivity" or "attract abundance." Later, I will discuss a beneficial alternative: cultivating helpful mind states.

Summary

Pain (and that guy) brought me to meditation. Reduced suffering keeps me here. I combine principles from ancient Buddhist teachings with my own movement experience to implement mindful movement. I tried many other practices. I only named a few. They either put a band-aid on the cause or attempted to divert my attention from it. By contrast, mindfulness approached it head-on, and for me, offered the most relief.

YOUR TURN: WHY YOU BOTHER

The next time you do your preferred movement form, choose an interval and an object of meditation. Before you begin your mindful movement, ask yourself what led you to choose this book. Begin to move and direct your mind to your object of meditation. If thoughts of why you picked up this book come to you while you're practicing, acknowledge them, allow them to float away like clouds, and gently bring your mind back to your object of meditation. Continue for whatever interval of time you choose.

In the next section, I will discuss the "body sensations" on which you focus your attention. Varied and plentiful, they offer lots of options for practice.

CHAPTER 4

SPLENDID BODY: SENSE GATES

The Art of Not Drowning

If I didn't stay present, I would drown. At least that's how it felt at age forty-nine as I crawled my way across a four-foot-deep Olympic pool. Determined to learn to swim before my fiftieth birthday, I'd signed up for lessons at a local health club. The friendly, eager instructor encouraged me to use fins, goggles, a swim cap—whatever it took to achieve my goal.

But she had to start the first lesson by convincing me to get in the pool. I don't like being cold, and I'm terrified of water. When I had to put my face in, my mind registered the shock of cold as deadly. Before I took a single stroke, she taught me how to turn my head to breathe while I was standing, holding onto the edge of the pool.

Eventually, with much practice, the kick, stroke, and breathing combined to form an activity much less elegant than what the people gliding past in other lanes were doing. But I propelled myself through the water just the same.

Meditation teaches us to be with thoughts and body sensations regardless of their quality. Years of practice kept me from screaming or drowning or simply getting out of the pool. Each stroke provided an opportunity to feel the water against my skin. Each breath was a chance to notice how inhaling feels from an unfamiliar position. And each kick offered the lesson of how relaxing was the key to power, especially in the pool.

That sounds miserable! Why put yourself through that?

Part of it *was* miserable. Sometimes the present moment sucks.

I could have quit. Nothing required me to stay. But we all know that a day will come when the moment sucks and we won't have the choice to get out of the pool. Grief. Physical pain. Sadness. Confusion. Anxiety. At some point, most of us will experience those intensely with no way out. Meditation trains us what to do when we can't escape. It reduces the suffering.

Did you learn to swim?

Yes, and no.

I can swim across an Olympic-size pool if it is only four feet deep. If I had continued swimming meditation, I could have honed my awareness and equanimity and learned to swim in water over my head. But time is limited, and I didn't enjoy it. For now, I'll stick to dry land.

Qualities of Sensation

When I was learning to swim, many of the moments seemed "bad." In truth, they were only unpleasant. But we humans tend to categorize experiences as good or bad. We go through each day thinking, "This is good. That's bad," on and on.

The words we use to describe our experiences matter. In this practice, rather than thinking of sensations as "good" or "bad," we label them as "pleasant," "unpleasant," or "neutral." Notice the difference? We're training our minds with everything we do, say, and think.

- Pleasant could potentially cause craving.
- Unpleasant could potentially cause aversion.
- Neutral could cause either, depending on your mind state.

As part of the "intention" I mentioned earlier, as you do these practices, stay awake to the words you use to describe your experience. Watch for any judgment that might arise. It's another way to grow in equanimity.

Using Your Five Senses

When you practice mindful movement meditation, the "experience" you choose to infuse with awareness and equanimity is made of real-time thoughts and body sensations. This chapter discusses body sensations. I start with body sensations because they are easier for most people to work with, especially beginners.

Body sensations include each of the five senses: sight, smell, taste, sound, and touch, including the breath. The senses are referred to as "gates" because experience flows through them. When you choose a body sensation as your object of meditation, that experience enters your consciousness through one of these five sense gates.

A tiny note of caution. I'm giving you a variety of options here and in future chapters. Please don't try all of the exercises at once. Start with the simplest and practice that for a time before moving to something else. Build your inner fitness as you go along.

Felt Sense

Touch, or "felt sense," is any sensation experienced in the body, including the breath and physical touch.

Breath

The breath is a "felt sense," a form of touch. I talk about the breath separately from other forms of touch because everyone breathes. That's why most meditation teachers start their instruction by telling students to focus on the breath. The breath is handy. It's always happening in the present moment, and focusing on the breath generally has a natural calming effect. This common denominator challenges any resistant part of the mind. It can't believably say, "I don't breathe."

The breath also offers an excellent object of focus for moving meditation. We tend to notice the breath even more when we move because activity makes the breath stronger and easier to sense. Movement might make the breath more mobile, ragged, or rough depending on the intensity of the exercise, all things we can notice. With practice, breath awareness has a natural calming effect that can improve performance.

When you use the breath as your object of meditation during movement, notice how the breath actually feels in real time. This differs from the way breath is used in other practices such as yoga. Here, you do not try to change the breath. You notice the breath exactly as it is without altering it. This goes for moving meditation as well.

Notice these four parts of the breath:

> The inhale
> A *turn* or brief pause before the exhale
> The exhale
> A *turn* or brief pause before the next inhale

At first, it may be easier to identify these four parts when you're sitting or slow walking. But once you become awake to them, you'll notice them when you're moving more quickly too.

Don't be discouraged if it's challenging to maintain your attention for all four parts of even one full breath. Most people find it challenging at first. Back when you began to do the movement form you now love, it was difficult. And it got easier. The same is true with focus. With practice, it will become more natural as well.

A note to people with anxiety: At first, focusing on the breath might make you nervous. Feel free to skip using the breath as your object of meditation until you grow more comfortable with the meditation process. Try using any of the other senses or body sensations. Or, if you want to ease into using the breath, lie on the floor with a book on your belly while tuning into your breath. That usually forces you to breathe from your diaphragm and does not induce the anxiety sometimes brought on by other types of breath meditation.

YOUR TURN: FEEL THE BREATH

The next time you exercise, before you begin to move, find the part of the breath that is most readily apparent to you. Often, this is the exhale. Try to extend that level of attention to all parts of the breath continuously.

Now, begin your movement form. As you do, watch the breath as though from within the body, feeling it come and go. Sense what it feels like and how it moves in and out. Experience the quality of the breath. Be aware if it is soft and gentle, raspy, hard, thin, or broad. Don't think about the breath, be in it. Feel it. Investigate it with your attention. Sense if there's any anxiety around the breath. Are you trying to control it? If so, can you be curious about it and let it be exactly as it is? Is the breath pleasant? Unpleasant? Neutral?

If you have trouble concentrating on the breath, note and label: inhale and exhale.

Especially at first, don't be concerned if you forget you're supposed to be focused on the breath. When you remember, simply bring your mind back to the breath. If you feel even one breath all the way through, give yourself a mental gold star. Do this exercise for whatever interval of time you choose.

Physical Touch and Reverberations

Body sensations also include physical touch: the touch of your clothes against your skin, a pain in your knee, or the feeling of a full bladder. A warm sensation in your chest, growing as you see something beautiful, or a cold prickle of fear if you hear a wild animal rustling along the trail are all body sensations. Any "feeling" in the body is a body sensation. Your skin, with 1,000 nerve endings every square inch, and your feet, with 200,000 nerve endings each, offer endless opportunities for body sensation focus.

These include the sensations at the bottoms of your feet, the shifting of your weight from side to side, and the way the air temperature feels against your skin.

Felt sense includes anything you handle in your movement practice, anything you feel such as the grip of your tennis racquet or golf club, your hand inside a glove, or the texture of a basketball.

If you don't use equipment, use your awareness of anything else in your body.

Remember that left foot meditation I do when I walk or run? There, I'm using "touch" or "felt sense" as my object of meditation. I attend to the sensation of my left foot placing itself on the ground, lifting off the ground, and hanging in the air in between. When my mind wanders, I gently bring it back.

Work with attention skills when you're getting to wherever you're going to exercise. Feel your hands on the steering wheel of the car, your grip on the pole or handle of the bus, or your hand turning the door handle as you walk out your front door. That preparation tunes you into the moment before your workout begins.

Felt sense also includes reverberations within the body that occur from an experience that comes in through one any of the sense gates. For example, if you see a beautiful flower through the visual field, you might also feel the edges of your lips turn up or the sting from a tear. Those reverberations are also "felt sensations." You feel them in your body in real time.

If your mind wanders or thoughts intrude, use the noting and labeling technique I explained before. Note the sensation you experience and label it.

A word for people who are not naturally proprioceptive (i.e., folks who live in their heads): This practice could be a revelation. The unfamiliarity might also bring up uncomfortable sensations. Not to worry. Recycle that discomfort. Please be patient with yourself. Practice with slow movement first. Be gentle with that part of your mind that freaks out when it feels your left foot for the first time. I promise it won't kill you.

YOUR TURN: FEEL TOUCH

The next time you're ready to begin your favorite movement form, before you start, choose some aspect of physical touch that's readily apparent to use as your object of meditation. Begin to move. During the move, focus your attention on the touch sensation you chose. Don't think about it or imagine it. Experience it from the inside. Get curious about it. Let your attention spread over it and sink into it. Is any part of it pleasant? When your mind wanders from that felt sense, gently bring your focus back to that felt experience. Do this exercise for whatever interval of time you choose.

YOUR TURN: NOTING AND LABELING PHYSICAL TOUCH

Doing the same "Feel Touch" exercise, if your thoughts distract you, give your chosen aspect of physical touch a label. Remember that "noting" is being aware of the touch, while the label is the name you've given it. For my left foot meditation, the sensations are anything in the foot, and I usually label them "foot" or "left."

When you select a sense of touch you'd like to work with and have chosen your label, start your activity. As you move, whenever you experience that particular felt sense, label it. "Grip" or "touch" or "left" or "shift" or "slide" or "bend" or "twist"—the options are endless. Do this exercise for whatever interval of time you choose.

Sight

For humans, the visual field, sight, is our most powerful sense. This makes sight very stimulating, which is why in sitting meditation, you might be instructed to close your eyes or keep them cast downward.

In most mindful movement, we keep our eyes open so we can see where we're going. We may use any aspect of things we see as an object of meditation, including color, shape, tone, and motion.

Color

I love to choose a color and notice it during my workout. Outdoors, I often choose green because it is so plentiful and easy to spot. In winter, I choose gray for the same reason.

I set out on my trek, dog at my side, and allow the color to enter my field of vision. A more free-floating awareness works best with vision movement meditation because I don't know what I'll see ahead of time. Since it's usually green, I can change to a more focused awareness when I see a large green patch such as a big tree or lawn. In winter, I can home in on a snow-covered lawn. But since I am moving, I don't keep my attention on that same spot for my entire workout.

When green catches my eye, I allow it to fill my vision, noting any shapes and textures within the green, perhaps the leaves or branches of a vine.

If I think, "Oh, that's green" or "Oh, there are branches," I let that drop. Instead, I allow the color to fill my vision, entering that sense gate of my eyes.

Because I am moving, that green will pass. If I see no green for a few moments, I sense that space, the absence of green, and calmly wait for green to appear again.

I might also note different shades, the vast variety of green where I live, including pale green, bright spring green, olive green, and dark—nearly black—green. I allow my mind to float over these things, not holding any of them, but simply letting them enter my visual field.

Motion

Tonight, on our walk, I chose to notice motion in my visual field. I watched for anything moving. It was an open-awareness practice. Opening my heart and mind to whatever might come allowed me to practice equanimity.

What did I see? Leaves moving in the wind. A car driving past on a side street. Then, the space of nothing moving after the car passed out of view (i.e., an experience of "gone"). A black and white cat flicking its tail at the pupperina. The pupperina's copper ears perking as the cat flicked its tail. Then, nothing. Stillness. It was 9 p.m. and dark. Next, I caught the intermittent flashes of the lighted Noxgear vest my dog Scarlet wears after dark, followed by the flashing of my own 360 Tracer vest. For three and a half miles, I let my awareness shift to whatever movement caught my eye. When nothing moved, I noticed spaciousness. And then, movement again.

I was not thinking about the movements I saw. I did not judge them. I noticed pleasant or unpleasant body sensations or thoughts if those arose, but I let the visual sensation of movement enter through my eyes. I allowed any other sensations or thoughts to arise and pass away.

When I became lost in thought—about what I might do tomorrow or even how I might write about tonight's experience—I remembered I had chosen this walk as a meditation. I gently brought my mind back to noticing movement.

Motion in Motion

I like to notice the motion that happens because I am moving. Here in central Ohio, it often gets icy, and I won't run outdoors. We moved the furniture (and my writing archive boxes) away from the basement walls to create a tiny oval "track." When I run there, I choose a color as my object of meditation. Recently, I chose orange. As I trotted around, I noticed the orange salt lamp, the dark rust of my mother's old chairs (the only ones the pupperina hasn't eaten), and an orange and black pin-on tail from a collection of costume items I use in the writing classes I teach.

After a mile, when I changed directions from clockwise to counterclockwise, I saw the orange exercise ball and then the orange on the side of the box my laptop came in. Each of these things appeared in my visual field, and then as I continued, they passed away.

When memories or judgments arose, I acknowledged those, then dropped them and returned my mind to the chosen color.

If my mind wandered too much as I noticed experiences of my chosen object of meditation, I labeled them: "orange," "orange," "orange."

Seeing Color

YOUR TURN: SEEING COLOR

Regardless of whether you do your chosen movement form
indoors or outdoors, if you have a normal range of vision, you will
see color. Before you begin your next workout, choose a color
as your object of meditation. Make it one you enjoy—no need to
torture yourself.

Begin your session and, as you move, stay awake to where you
see the color you selected. As it appears in your visual field, notice
that. As it passes, notice that. Also notice any emotional states or
preferences that arise as you see the color appear and disappear
from your field of vision.

If your thoughts intrude, when you see the color, label it.

Sound

Today, on an easy jog with Scarlet the pupperina, I noticed the autumn
wind rustling through the trees. I had originally intended to focus on
sadness, confusion, and brooding feelings about a highly charged situation. I
intended to allow some drama (my own and that of others) and my flash-
bright anger over it to flood my senses to see what might resolve while my
feet pounded the pavement.

But that wind caught my attention. I dropped my original plan and shifted
my awareness to those leaves. I noticed my impulse to imagine them in my
mind's eye, to "see" them (but not really). I noticed that and returned to
pure sound.

As we jogged along, taking it easy, letting my body rest during what felt like a stressful time, I continued to let any sounds of the wind in the trees fill my ears. And that's what it felt like, the sound filled my ears. Mostly pleasant, a crackly crinkle sound as the leaves began to die in preparation for their annual shedding. Again, the image of dried leaves popped into my head. I acknowledged the visual image and let that thought pass on its own.

Soon, my ears again filled with the pure sound of leaves in wind on a fall day. When the wind slowed, the sound grew faint. I did my best not to strain to hear it, but let it go as it naturally did, practicing equanimity around the quiet. When the wind died down completely, I noticed the space left by the quiet—the absence of sound and relative silence. When the wind started again, I noticed the wavelike quality of it coming and going, arising, doing its little sound dance, and passing away.

Note how I limited my object of meditation to one thing: the sound of the wind in the trees, more specifically, the sound of the wind in drying leaves, a very distinct sound and one I find pleasant. I also noticed impermanence, the changing of the sound. And I did my best to infuse what I was hearing, as well as my reaction to it, with equanimity. It was clear I preferred to hear the sound, but I noticed that and let that go, too. I returned to reality, to what existed in that moment, including my own desire. And, as is often the case when I practice, the emotional flurry that had consumed me earlier calmed as I carried out this meditation.

When Sound Is Painful

Even if the sound is painful, that irritation can be transformed into meditative practice. On an early morning trail run, I felt my body tense as I heard the slosh, slosh, slosh of ice in a fellow runner's hydration vest. Every slosh sent ripples of unpleasant sensations flooding through my body. I tightened and my brain began to judge. "Why hadn't she burped the bladder so it wouldn't slosh?"

I have misophonia, an intermittent phobia triggered by repetitive sounds. Some days that sound wouldn't bother me at all. On another day, overwhelmed by unpleasant body sensations, I would fall back and let her get ahead, out of earshot.

But that morning, I decided to use the experience as practice. She's a friend, relatively new to running. It was an opportunity.

I relaxed my body and mind and let the slosh, slosh, slosh flood through me. It still rattled me, but it became a challenge to hear every bit of it. I laser-focused and opened to it, examining it with the microscope of awareness. No longer resisting, I allowed the sound to pass through me. Zen calls this "Becoming the sound." Interesting and less painful, the miles rolled by.

Scent

Smell or scent is another sense gate available as an object of meditation. Scent evokes memory. Those memories are thoughts I will discuss more later. Be aware of the difference between the scent itself and a memory, which is probably an image or inner monologue. Instead, notice any place in the body where the scent resonates. That would be a felt sense rather than a smell, but it is important to notice.

One of my favorite seasons to use scent meditation, or "sniff meditation" as I like to call it, since I often run with my sniffing dog, is during the spring when the lilacs bloom. I start out and let my awareness float, noticing any scent that arises. Spring in central Ohio smells fresh and green. This loamy, bright scent evokes pleasant body sensations and visual images of the green fields where I grew up.

As I run, I look (with my nose) for lilacs. Often, I smell them before I see them. Does purple have a smell? If so, it's lilac. I take care not to crave the scent, but to let it waft to me and let it go when it is behind me.

This one is a bit trickier, because I do want to smell lilacs. I enjoy them so much. And so, I make any craving part of my practice, noting the almost painful feeling of hoping I pass a lilac bush, and also a slight tinge of sadness when I'm far enough away that the scent fades to memory. And the memory, too, becomes the practice.

Taste

The final sense gate is taste, sensations that arise in the mouth, whether from things we put in our mouth or flavors in the mouth that emanate from our bodies.

Anyone who does any kind of movement practice must fuel the machine (a.k.a., the body). And much of what this practice entails, perhaps the point of meditation in general, is to learn to take this into every part of our lives. One way is to meditate while you eat.

Follow these basic instructions to meditate on taste:

Start with a simple food you enjoy but won't scarf down in one bite. Take a small portion and sit down to eat it, preferably at a table. It might help if you need to eat it with silverware. Having the chance to place the silver on the table can be part of the practice.

Cut off a portion smaller than you might normally eat. As you do this, notice any thoughts that arise. These might be judgments about the process, about yourself, or about the food. Simply notice.

Put the portion onto your fork or spoon.

Slowly begin to lift the food to your mouth. As you do so, notice what happens in your mouth, your body, and your mind. Again, sense if judgment arises. Also note if these thoughts or sensations are pleasant, unpleasant, or neutral.

Put the food in your mouth, but don't chew or swallow. Let it sit on your tongue.

This is why it's helpful to use food that you're not likely to gobble down. Especially when you're first learning to meditate on taste, you need to practice slowly to get the full experience.

With the food in your mouth, sense it fully. What does it actually taste like? What does it feel like? Notice the texture. What flavors do you experience and where? And does anything radiate in your mouth or even through your body?

Then slowly begin to chew or swallow. Notice, notice, notice. Are there sensations? What quality do they have—pleasant, unpleasant, or neutral? Does anything move or change? Does anything radiate? Do you "feel" the experience in other parts of your body? Do thoughts arise?

Finally, once you have completely chewed and swallowed the food, notice any lingering sensations in your mouth, on your tongue, your gums, your throat. Does this flow into the rest of your body? You might experience an aftertaste, or after-sensations, echoes of the food.

There are no wrong answers. It's all about the experience, about being in reality. And no, you don't need to eat this way all the time!

When you eat, you will probably notice all of the senses and have many thoughts. This is why eating is so pleasurable. It literally floods all the sense gates, often with positive sensations. You'll have pleasant body sensations and anticipatory feelings as you see the food, cut it, bring it to your mouth. The same will happen when you smell the food. The texture of the food in your mouth may also cause sensations and thoughts to arise. And who doesn't remember the sound of their teeth piercing the skin of an apple? What a hit of sensation!

I only mentioned taste sensations in the above instructions. But any sensation from any sense gate, including thoughts (stay tuned) can be your object when eating. If you begin thinking, acknowledge the thought and gently bring your mind back to the sensations of taste.

During a long run, when I eat or drink during the workout, I focus on taste as my object of meditation. But even if you aren't eating or drinking, notice any taste or the absence of taste.

When Your Body Doesn't Feel Splendid

Anxiety, depression, panic attacks, paranoia, and other mental health situations can cause us to feel ungrounded and spacey. Focusing awareness on the body with equanimity brings us back to the present moment, to the ground of being, right here in our bodies. The body is a weight, an anchor. We carry it around all day. Being present to the body can bring us a sense of calm and security that may help with the mental health issues.

But body awareness isn't always pleasant. The body can feel uncomfortable, the anxiety too painful, the paranoia too severe. The depression may seem so heavy it feels as if we will drown.

During the time I describe as "the year everyone died," my unpleasant thoughts and body sensations grew dangerous. When first my niece, then several other friends and family members, including my father-in-law and eventually my mother, all died in the span of eleven months, the physical ache of grief and depression generated thoughts like, "What's the point?" and, "No one would miss me if I weren't here," and, "I can't take this anymore."

Even in those darkest of times, meditation helped me see those thoughts and body sensations for what they actually are: processes, not solid objects. That awareness unhooked me from the downward spiral and reduced the suffering brought on by these life and mental health challenges.

Focusing on my body scares me. What should I do?

If attending to your body sensations causes distress, try limiting your focus to your hands or feet. Many strong emotions arise in the chest and belly. Emotional sensations from the body's center sometimes overwhelm even experienced meditators.

If focusing on just the hands or feet feels scary, try sight, smell, sound, or taste instead. Choosing to switch it up this way does not mean you have given in to distraction. Rather, you are observing reality and choosing a more effective method, one that brings more joy than pain. We have options and can make choices. Mindful experience of the splendid body is ours to use.

Summary

To ground the mind in the body, use any of the five body "sense gates" as your object of meditation in the same way one might ground the mind in the breath while sitting. When you're first trying mindful movement meditation, choose one sense gate. Stay with it for a bit until you gain confidence in that method of practice.

The sensations have three qualities: pleasant, unpleasant, or neutral. Again, as you learn, choose one of these qualities and notice it until your practice builds. Once you have more concentration, broaden your awareness to notice any mix of these qualities you might experience.

Next, I'll talk about the mind and thinking. Thoughts that arise during movement practice are part of your experience, a thing to notice, and another opportunity for mindful movement.

CHAPTER 5

TRICKY MIND: WORKING WITH THOUGHTS

What to Do with Your Thoughts While You Move

I can't meditate. My mind is too active. I can't stop thinking.

If I had a dollar (or even a dime) for every time I've heard that, I'd be set financially for life. The prevailing myth that meditation requires you to still the mind is pervasive and false. When you meditate, you don't try to calm your mind or stop thoughts, you work with them. As a result of meditation, thinking may slow, but that's not the point. Rather, as you know, the point of meditation is to bring ourselves into the present moment. With practice, we can use our thoughts for that purpose.

Why do you call it the "tricky" mind?

Thoughts are seductive, entertaining, powerful. We easily get caught in thought, hop on the thought train, and ride it all the way to the wrong station. Meditation teaches us to let each thought arise, do its little dance, and pass away. Because thinking is so sticky and seductive, many meditation teachers do not offer thought meditation to beginning students. The lure of the thinking rabbit hole can be a powerful waste of time.

A racing mind can cause pain to the point of suffering. Most people daydream, worry, or plan much of the time. Our thoughts are rarely in the present. Until we begin to bring our attention into the moments we inhabit, noticing how thoughts come and go, we may not even realize how busy the mind can be. And we might not have felt the discomfort our thinking causes. Ouch. No wonder people don't want to meditate.

If meditation doesn't stop thoughts and thinking can cause suffering, what the heck do I do?

You ask such good questions!

As you learn mindful movement meditation, you can choose thoughts as your "object of meditation," the thing on which you place your attention. This differs vastly from ordinary thinking.

Thoughts are not your enemy. They are part of experience. You attend to thoughts the same way you would any other aspect of experience, by infusing them with awareness and equanimity.

Instead of letting the mind wander, you notice thoughts, let them come and go, rise and fall, but don't identify with them or get caught in them. With practice, your mind will settle.

Please know that using thoughts as your object of meditation requires powerful concentration and strong intent. Not willpower: Focus. Not control: Intention. Meditation on thought requires fierce curiosity and a strong intention to see and experience reality as it is. It requires you to be eager to return to the present moment.

Two Types of Thoughts

Before we explore techniques for using thoughts as the object of meditation, let's talk about the two types of thoughts: auditory and visual. Auditory thoughts are words or sentences you "hear" in your mind. Visual thoughts include images you "see" in your mind. Words are like radio and images like silent movies. Both may occur at the same time.

If, while doing your movement meditation, you simply notice that thoughts come in those two varieties, you'll be ahead of many people when it comes to awareness. The general population, thinking all the time, is asleep to these classifications. Start there, noticing that thoughts come in two forms.

Once you have made yourself familiar with the two types of thoughts, things get super interesting (for meditation geeks, at least).

Auditory Thoughts

The first category of thought is auditory or sound thoughts. You hear snippets of sentences, repeated words, music you heard or made up, or conversations in your mind. The classic earworm song that sticks in your head is an example of a very intrusive and repetitive auditory thought.

Similar to "image thoughts," these auditory thoughts may be recognizable or may not. They may shift from a song you know into one you don't, then into something completely unrecognizable. They might be static or a single sound but will often move and change.

You can "see" words as visual representations, but those are image thoughts. When you "hear" words, those are auditory thoughts. Notice the difference? It's subtle. To quote Shinzen, "Subtle is significant,"[19]

---

19 Shinzen Young, "Meditation: Escaping into Life—An Interview with Shinzen Young by Michael Toms." December 7, 2016. www.shinzen.org/wp-content/uploads/2016/12/art_escape.pdf.

Visual Thoughts

The second category of thought is visual. Within this category, the mind offers endless possibilities. You know how your TV has 3,000 channels but nothing's on? The mind has a billion channels. Something's always on. Let's look more closely.

You might see a person's face, an image of a car you used to drive, a plate of food, or a scene from a movie or television. Those images might be vivid and real and in color. These recognizable images might be static for a minute, but often they move and change.

Or you might see fuzzy or vague images you can't quite make out. They could be black and white or in color. They might be static for a bit, a solid color or one pattern, but often they will move and change. "Image thoughts" may switch from recognizable to impressionistic.

Visual thoughts are easiest to spot when you meditate with your eyes closed. Since you probably keep your eyes open during movement meditation (safety first), visual thoughts are less likely, but not impossible. Have you ever been in the middle of a long, repetitious workout when a scene from a movie scrolled through your mind? If you see the characters or backdrop, those are visual thoughts.

People tend to have a preferred mode of thought: auditory or visual. As a writer, I tend to think by hearing words or inner sounds rather than in images. My painter friend's thoughts arise in images. Notice yours.

How to Meditate on Thought

Even though our goal in meditation is to be in the present moment and accept it exactly as it is without judgment, the present moment may include busy, chatty, annoying thoughts we can't stop. Rather than try to stop thoughts, we create conditions that allow the mind to calm on its own. We invite a quiet mind; we don't force it. Trying to strong-arm thoughts to slow often has the opposite effect. Instead, we train and encourage the mind.

How do you create this encouraging environment when thoughts are so tricky?

Exactly the same way you meditate on body sensations: Infuse the experience, in this case, your thoughts, with awareness and equanimity.

Let's say you've finished a game and you're walking to your car. You have chosen thought as your object of meditation. As you walk along, notice your mind. It might seem like a blank slate. Scan your mind, or let your mind be completely open. Don't look for anything.

At some point, a thought will arise. It may present itself like a seed, merely a bud of a thought, as opposed to a full-blown image or phrase. Use the concentration you are building to stay present to that thought. And use the equanimity you are building to allow that thought to blossom or fade away, without giving it any additional energy. The thought may encounter your awareness and disappear, leaving you with a calm, blank state of mind. Other times the thought will grow and grow in your awareness. Your job is only to notice. See it or hear it.

Thoughts are a sixth "sense gate," a sixth way in addition to our five senses through which information flows to us. And while we use the same technique with thought as we use with body sensations, working with thought requires more awareness and equanimity. Don't be discouraged if you find it difficult to work with thoughts as your object of meditation, especially while doing movement meditation. If you're moving through space, it might be difficult to track thinking and at the same time stay physically safe.

Continue to use body sensations, including the breath, as your object. Acknowledge any thoughts that arise, and repeatedly return to the breath or body sensation. Build your concentration. Once you become confident in your ability to focus, try working with thought. You may also need personal instruction in how to deal skillfully with thoughts that continue to intrude when you try to focus elsewhere. Remain aware of your surroundings and do your best.

YOUR TURN: AUDITORY AND VISUAL THOUGHTS

Because thoughts are sticky and tricky, until you've strengthened your concentration, don't attempt this exercise while doing a complex activity. Rather, take a walk or even a hike! As you move, place your awareness on the breath. Use it like a base or anchor, a safe place to rest between thoughts. Keep your mind on your breath until you notice a thought arise. Get curious. Is the thought an image, or do you hear words? Do your best to remain neutral, open, and interested. Equanimity makes the thought less sticky and keeps you from following the thought out into the not-meditating atmosphere. Let the thought do its little dance and dissipate. If you get caught in it, don't fret. Just bring your awareness back to that friendly base—your breath. Continue to keep your awareness on your breath until another thought arises. Again, notice what type of thought it is. Let it rise and fall. Continue this for as long as you wish.

YOUR TURN: PAST AND FUTURE THOUGHTS

As with the "Auditory and Visual Thoughts" exercise, until you feel comfortable with your ability to focus, choose a simple movement during which to try this exercise.

During a walk, place your awareness on a simple body sensation. Use it like a base or anchor the same way you did in the previous exercise. Keep your mind on that body sensation until a thought arises. When one does, notice whether it is a thought about the past, present, or future. If it is a thought about either the past or the future, acknowledge it, then bring your mind back to that body sensation. If the thought is about the present, notice as it rises and falls. When it has passed, bring your mind back to your object of meditation. Continue for whatever interval you wish.

Planning, Remembering, and Worry

When I suggested staying in the moment to a good friend who is quite the planner, a self-proclaimed control freak, she confided that she adores making schedules and project templates and imagining setting things in motion. "That's lovely," I told her. I too love to plan, especially planning travel to races in different states or to see presidential libraries with Ed.

But we do that planning right now. We sit at desks and hop on websites. We call the airlines or get on the app. We're not there yet. That all happens later. The more present we can be, and the more aware of our thoughts and feelings while we make plans, the more compassion we have for the possibly overworked travel agent, hotel reservation specialist, or car rental agent; the more flexible we can be about the options, the better both the planning and possibly the trip, will go.

Planning is in the future. Remembering is in the past. Mindfulness is in the present. Now. Here. Be.

We can't plan for the future in the future. And we're not in the past when we're thinking about the past. We're here. We make the plans for tomorrow, today. We remember things we did or said in the past, now. It's all happening now. There isn't any yesterday or tomorrow. There is only now.

What about planning and remembering that happens during my movement meditation practice? Will the mindfulness police come along and give me a ticket?

Of course not.

You are practicing. If you choose an object of meditation and thoughts of the future arise, whether planning or worrying or simply daydreaming, treat them as such: thoughts. They are not good or bad, and neither are you for thinking them. And yes, they are a distraction. Notice them, and notice that you have drifted from your object of meditation. Notice the power in having remembered. Then gently bring your mind back to whatever you have chosen to observe during that particular practice session.

Treat memories the same way. There's not much more lovely than a sweet memory. And, if you are doing a movement meditation, that memory is probably not your chosen object of meditation. Train the mind to let the memory go.

As a writer, I record these plans or memories, especially if they relate to my current project. I use a digital recorder app on my phone. Another friend carries index cards. If you must preserve these, do so, then return to your practice. You might have remembered it later anyway, but recording it calms the mind, letting you return to your movement meditation practice.

You know another thing that's not in the present? Worry. You might not put worry in the same category as planning or remembering since you probably already know it's unproductive. But worry, like planning and remembering, is simply a form of thinking. And it is not in the present. When you worry, your mind imagines a negative future. Unpleasant memories may trigger worry. A memory of something you don't want to happen again can trigger fears of the future. That unpleasant cycle can roll around and around, especially if you have a history of trauma.

Use the same skills with worry as with planning, remembering, or any other thought pattern. Worry can be more unpleasant. It stirs more emotions, making it stickier and more difficult to release, but the process is the same. As soon as you notice you are worrying—that your mind has moved away from your chosen object of meditation—acknowledge the thought, then gently bring your mind back and return to practice.

If worry persists, add another step. Thank your mind. Worry may arise because an ancient part of your mind, one sometimes referred to as reptilian,[20] believes it needs to warn and protect you. While a more developed part of the mind knows worry is counterproductive, that older part does not. So, thank it. Bow in gratitude. Then, remind it you are meditating. Ask it to trust you while you practice. Tell it you hear what it is trying to tell you. Then, again, with the utmost gentleness, but also firmness, bring your awareness back to your object of meditation.

Mental Health

People with mental health challenges have extra wrinkles in the thinking process. Mental health symptoms add an extra layer or filter that may lead to depressed, anxious, obsessive, recurring, or leaden thoughts. Those with mental health issues work with a mind that is extra active, extra inactive, or both.

All minds are tricky. It's just a matter of degree. Depending on how you experience thoughts, thinking is either a seductive, slippery slope with a sticky trap at the bottom or a window into the nature of consciousness. This is why it's important, particularly if you have such issues, to have guidance, a meditation teacher and/or therapist to help you navigate these waters.

20 Robert K. Naumann, Janie M. Ondracek, Samuel Reiter, Mark Shein-Idelson, Maria Antonietta Tosches, Tracy M. Yamawaki, and Gilles Laurent. "The reptilian brain," www. ncbi.nlm.nih.gov/pmc/articles/PMC4406946/ (April 20, 2015).

Summary

Be clear about the nature of thought. The human mind uses thought to model reality, but thoughts are not reality itself. We are not our thoughts, and we don't have to believe everything we think. Some thoughts are useful. Some are not. No need to quiet the mind. We let it quiet itself.

We can select thoughts as our object for movement practice the same way we use body sensations. While thoughts may be more seductive and trickier, once you've built stronger concentration skills, thoughts offer insight into everyday experience.

The mind is like the sky. Some days it is clear. Other days, clouds fill it. The clouds are not the sky. They simply pass through. When we meditate, we can't always see the clear sky of our mind, but with enough practice, we can let the clouds pass. And regardless of how clouded with thoughts the mind may be, we always know that clear blue sky is there.

In the chapter ahead, I'll introduce additional ways to practice beyond simple awareness. The options are limitless.

CHAPTER 6

ADVANCED AWARENESS TECHNIQUES

In Chapter Two, "How to Meditate While You Move," I set out the fourth step in meditating while you move: "Place your awareness on the object of meditation." I explained how to direct attention to a particular sensation (e.g., experiencing the sensations in my left foot), how to note and label body sensations, and how to use counting for focus. Once you have practiced those techniques for long enough to develop some meditative awareness, you may want to explore the more "advanced" techniques in this chapter.

Scanning

Scanning is a popular awareness technique in which you move your awareness through a variety of objects of meditation. You can scan for anything entering the "sense gates" including sensations, the other senses, or thoughts.

Scanning the Body

The most common scan technique is the "body scan." A body scan uses the felt sense of touch. Often a guided meditation, you move the attention from one part of the body to another, "scanning" the body with your attention. Going back to our camera analogy, a "scan" is exactly as it sounds, except the "camera" (your attention) is placed on one specific body part at a time. Here's one to try:

YOUR TURN: STATIONARY BODY SCAN

Start by paying attention to your toes. Let your awareness sink deeply into them. What do you feel there? Are there pleasant or unpleasant sensations? Simply notice them. Remain open to them no matter what quality the sensations may have. Stay with your toes for a few seconds.

Next, move to the rest of your left foot. Focus your full attention there. What sensations arise when you do that? Be awake to those. Let the sensory impressions do whatever dance they may do as you observe. Stay with your foot for a few seconds.

As you scan, ideas and connections may arise. This is normal. Gently bring your attention back to the body part where you left off.

Continue this meditation through various parts of your body from the bottom to the top. When you reach the top of your head, intentionally move your awareness back down your body, part by part, again. Your interval in this exercise is however long it takes to move your awareness from your feet to your head and then back down.

YOUR TURN: MOVING BODY SCAN

Use this same mode of awareness—scanning—in movement meditation. As you move, slowly sweep the camera up and down the body, gradually noting any sensations.

Begin your movement practice. Place your awareness on your left foot. Settle your mind on your foot as you allow your attention to drop in. Get curious. Notice any sensations. Let your attention soak into those sensations. Keep your attention on your foot for at least a minute.

When you feel ready, move your awareness to your left ankle. Allow your attention to settle there. Do any sensations arise? What is "ankle?" What does "ankle" feel like? Allow your attention to stay with your ankle for at least a minute.

Next, move up to your shin and calf. Let your mind sink into that area. Open your mind to it exactly as it is. If you feel a preference, notice that. Stay awake, but relaxed.

When your mind wanders, gently bring it back to the part of your body you were last scanning. This is normal. Give yourself a tiny mental pat for remembering to return.

Continue moving through each part of your body with this mode of scanning awareness until you reach the top of your head and, if you like, travel back down again with your awareness. That is your interval.

Note that it is fine to use the right foot throughout, or to alternate sides either during one meditation period or from one to the next if you like. I have a personal preference for my left foot due to my health history. Do what works best with your body/mind.

For a full, guided, body scan, visit my website, www.nitasweeney.com.

Scanning Other Senses

You can scan other senses as well. If you have chosen the visual field, scan your surroundings. Use direction: left to right or vice versa, and straight ahead. Slowly take in one image after another.

Sound works, too. Open your awareness to sounds by direction. Listen to the right, then left, then center. Listen ahead or behind.

If you have a strong sense of smell or are in an area with a lot of scents, work with that. You don't need to sniff hard. Simply allow any scents to waft into your nose.

With taste, if you sip a sports drink or eat a power bar, scan for the flavor. Then, scan for the aftereffects. Sweep your mind from left to right across your tongue.

Be awake to any tendency to grasp at pleasant sensations or repel unpleasant ones. Note that some sensations are neutral.

Scanning builds focus and insight while heightening body awareness. Scanning can release tension and resistance, helping to bring us into the present moment in the body to overcome any mind/body split. Scanning requires focus in order to stay attuned to one part of the body, as well as to remember to move on while other thoughts and body sensations might call out. As you scan, ideas and connections may arise. This is normal. Celebrate remembering, and gently bring your attention back to the body part you last scanned.

Widening Focus

When I first began to run, that "wonky ankle" would swell. It rarely hurt during the run, but it ached after. I checked with a doctor I trust to make sure I wasn't injuring myself, then turned my attention during my post-run walks with Morgan to the sensations of a swollen ankle.

Unlike sharp pain, these mildly unpleasant sensations spread through my ankle, into my foot, and up my leg. When I chose "wonky ankle" as my object, I broadened my focus, allowing awareness to wander through my ankle, foot, shin, and calf. This wider focus, like widening the lens of a camera, allowed me to "see" more of the process. I still limited my focus to the ankle, but with a wider view than I mentioned before.

With continued development of your concentration, widen that focus of attention further, spreading it across your body, even into the world around you. Your eyes see far beyond your body, several miles ahead depending on your vision and the time of day. Your ears capture sounds in a large range. Choose this wider focus of attention and attend to whatever comes in through any of those five "sense gates."

The ability to open to this wider sense of awareness may bring insight about the nature of the world. Broad awareness may increase your enjoyment, offering a sense of freedom as you take in sensory beauty. It encourages an experience of oneness—the realization you are part of a larger whole.

As you try this, take care not to become scattered. You still need focus and concentration. You are simply expanding the awareness.

Also, be aware of the tendency to default to what is easy. There's no harm in building on your strengths, but once in a while, do the hard thing. If you're drawn to a broad focus, once in a while bring your awareness in and focus on one spot. Likewise, if you love that deep, sharp focus, try the opposite just to see what it is like. Do what comes naturally, but also push yourself a teensy bit to try what's tough. We really can do hard things.

YOUR TURN: WIDENING AWARENESS OF VISION

This exercise is best done either alone or with a practice partner who understands your mindful movement practice so you can tailor your workout accordingly. And remember, safety first.

Begin your movement. As you move, notice what you see directly in front of you, neither left nor right. Stay with that narrow focus of vision.

After a few minutes, allow your vision to expand. Begin to pay attention to things that might be in the periphery. They will not be as sharply defined as what is directly in front of you, but you will still be able to see them. Notice any frustration or straining at trying to see them better. Relax into the images exactly as they are.

After a few more minutes, allow your vision to relax. Let your eyes adjust to taking in anything above or below, left or right, and in front of you all at the same time. Do your best to relax into this unfamiliar type of seeing.

Any time your mind wanders, gently bring your focus back to the sharpest vision, usually what's directly in front of you. That sharp focus helps you regain concentration. Once you have refocused, you can again broaden your vision awareness. Do this for whatever interval you like.

Free-Floating Awareness

The next mode of awareness is "free-floating." Returning to the camera analogy, in this type of focus, point the camera at the first thing that draws your attention. You see a beautiful flower. Focus on it, taking your time to thoroughly see it before clicking the shutter. Even then, linger, letting the full image burn into your retinas. Only when you have finished do you move the camera to the next thing you see. Do this for the entire meditation session, slowly moving from thing to thing as you practice.

The hazard here is scattered attention. If you haven't trained your mind to focus, this session could turn into a series of distractions and not be effective. Be sure to stay with each object for at least a few seconds. Respect it. Sense it fully. Give it its due. Only then should you move on.

Once you have developed enough concentration to use thought as your object of meditation, you can choose which type of thought on which to place your awareness. With strong focus, you can do free-floating awareness. As thoughts bubble up in your consciousness, move your attention to whichever thought is most prominent, regardless of which type of thought it may be. Especially with thought, beware of the tendency to space out, even if the thoughts come rapidly.

YOUR TURN: FREE-FLOATING AWARENESS OF THE BREATH.

Begin your movement practice. Place your attention inside the breath, and remove any tendency to push or pull on it. Let it go in and out. Sense if it is shallow or deep. Notice if it increases in frequency or becomes less frequent. Feel the body parts involved in the breath and how they react to the in breath and the out breath. Do this for whatever interval you like.

YOUR TURN: FREE-FLOATING AWARENESS OF SENSATION

Begin your movement practice. Allow your attention to be drawn to whatever body sensation first arises in your consciousness. A sensation might yammer for your attention. Turn to that. Drop your attention deeply into it. Stay with it. Then, when it feels finished, move on to the next sensation you notice. Do this for whatever interval you like.

Touring the Senses

In *5-Minute Mindfulness: Walking*,[21] Douglas Baker offers another way of working with awareness that he calls "Touring the Senses." With this technique, Baker slowly moves his attention from one sense to the next while he walks. The process isolates sensations coming in from one particular sense gate and calms the barrage of sensory input. Once you have familiarized yourself with each of the sense gates, a tour could add variety to your practice.

Mindful Moments

Instead of staying with an object of meditation for any sustained period of time, another option is to intensely focus on one sensation for a brief period. Shinzen Young calls these "Mindful Microhits."

Shinzen specifically calls this type of short-interval meditation practice "Micro Practice."

His instructions state:

> "Micro Practice: Attention: All attention on technique. Duration: Under 10 minutes, i.e., you give yourself 'microhits' during the day; 30 seconds here, 3 minutes there (emphasis must be quality over quantity; if need be, use spoken labels to assure this)."[22]
>
> —Shinzen Young

While it might not seem like this would be effective, many studies support the effectiveness of even these small bursts of meditative practice. My

---

21   Douglas Baker, *5-Minute Mindfulness: Walking* (Beverly: Fair Winds Press, 2017), 44.

22   Shinzen Young "An Outline of Practice" May 2014, updated August 2016. www.shinzen.org/an-outline-of-practice.

cursory review of brief mindfulness abstracts from scientific research shows that as little as five minutes of mindfulness can have a positive impact and lessen suffering.[23]

Of all the techniques, this is the one most likely to spill over into the rest of your life. When you learn to attend fully to an experience in a short burst of concentration during your movement, you will naturally begin to do the same thing with experiences throughout your day.

YOUR TURN: MINDFUL MICROHITS

Begin your movement. Allow a body sensation to present itself to you. When it does, focus all of your attention on it completely. Relax around it, and allow it to move, change, or disappear altogether. Don't chase it. Only notice what happens. Keep your awareness on it for as long as it remains, up to five minutes. After it has passed, allow your body to offer another sensation. Repeat this process throughout your selected interval.

Advanced Breath and Counting

Additional ways to use the breath as the object of meditation:

Remember the four parts of the breath: the inhale, the turn, the exhale, and the pause before the next in breath. Some people find their minds

---

23   Nita Sweeney "Bibliography for 'No Time to Meditate? Try a "Micro-hit" of Mindfulness.' " nitasweeney.com/2021/07/bibliography-for-no-time-to-meditate-try-a-micro-hit-of-mindfulness.

wander during *the turn*. For others, *the pause* opens a door to thoughts and distraction.

YOUR TURN: COUNT EACH FULL BREATH

I previously suggested counting the inhales and exhales separately. For more of a challenge, count each full breath: "one" on the in breath, turn, exhale, pause. "Two" on the in breath, turn, exhale, pause. Count each full breath from one to ten. When you get to ten, count backward to one. Any time you lose count, begin again. Do this for whatever interval of time you like. This requires more concentration, and you may need to build up to it by using the first method of breath counting.

Movement can be tied to breath. This works best in movement forms that include repetitive actions and where you choose the pace. Change the movement to match your breath, not vice versa. Some yoga practices ask you to manipulate the breath, to time it with your movement. Here, you do the opposite.

Let's take walking as an example. Before you begin to walk, notice your breath in your body. Find the place where it is most easily recognizable: the place you sense it most readily, where it is most apparent. After an exhale, wait through the pause. On the inhale, take a step, then on the exhale, take another step. Or try it with just one foot, the left foot for example. On the inhale, lift your left foot, on the exhale, place it on the ground. On the next inhale, lift your right foot, on the exhale, place it on the ground. Move along a straight line in this way.

I use a similar technique with running by tying cadence (footfalls) to my breath. I find the natural place my breath falls in alignment with my foot strikes. Three breaths in, four breaths out, repeat. The number of breaths with each foot turnover will vary for each individual and your particular fitness on that day. Some days I only need three breaths per foot strike; on other days, four.

If you are dancing, do this with an arm swing or a twirl. Notice your breath and move your body in time with your breathing.

YOUR TURN: MATCH STEPS TO BREATH

While walking, match your steps to your breath: one breath for one step or one breath for two steps. Change the movement to match the breath. Find the pace that works for you. Do this for whatever interval you like. This builds concentration. Plus, you may experience frustration, another important thing to observe.

YOUR TURN: ADVANCED COUNTING

Ed learned this one-to-ten walking practice at a retreat in Santa Fe. It's fabulous for building both body awareness and concentration.

Begin to walk. On your first step, count one. Second and third step, count one, two. Fourth, fifth, and sixth step, count one, two, three, and so on up to ten, then back down. Again, when your mind wanders, begin again at one. Do this for whatever interval you like. If you feel discouraged, don't fret. This one also requires great concentration.

Use What Arises

Now that you have learned a wider variety of awareness techniques, another splendid thing about meditation becomes clear: you can use what's handy,

whatever aspect of experience occurs. You may set an intention to count
your breath during Jazzercise, but a few minutes into class, a mild arm
cramp draws your attention. It's not deep enough to worry or stop you, but
the sensation distracts.

Earlier in your meditation journey, you might not have developed the inner
fitness to return your attention to the breath. You might not have even
noticed your attention shifting from your breath to the pain. But now, having
developed those skills, you will remember. Choose whether to remain
with the breath or to change your object of meditation and investigate
the unpleasant sensations. Making that choice develops your calm and
concentration even more.

In sitting meditation, the teacher may encourage you to let the body ask
three times before you shift your position. Whether it's an itchy nose, knee
pain, or a numb hip—you notice, and return to the breath. The third time
the sensation arises, you choose. It is intentional. Tell yourself, "I choose to
move my awareness." That new spot becomes your focus.

Do this with your movement meditation. Choose the object of meditation
and when (or if) to shift your awareness. Let your mind ask three times.
The first two times, return to the original object. After the third time,
choose whether to make that your object of meditation. Make that mental
switch intentional.

Use what arises. You started with the breath, but that mild pain arose. Let it
ask a few times, showing it your intention. After the third "ask," you choose
whether to shift your attention. If you change objects, sink into the new
one as deeply as you might have the breath. It's your object now. This is an
aspect of free-floating awareness, free but still mindful.

Using what arises with intention makes meditation even more adaptable. It
trains you to go with the flow. You have that choice to shift gears. You don't
have to stop meditating or try to control it or escape from it. Dive into the

experience that presents itself in the moment. No need to fight anything, especially yourself. Be with reality, with what is.

Taking the Wrong Medicine

Shinzen often talks about the temptation to do what's easy or comes naturally. He calls it, "taking the wrong medicine." If for example you prefer guided workouts, a broad focus of attention, or listening to music during movement meditation, nothing is inherently wrong with those things. But what happens when your music player dies or when you're pushing yourself hard (in a safe way) and the intense mental effort requires focused attention? You already know this, but a day will come when there is nothing between you and a huge wall of suffering except how well you have trained your mind.

This is why you might want to work on things that don't come naturally.

In many areas of life—business, relationships, hobbies—it makes sense to hone skills around your natural talents. You're already ahead of the crowd. Not so with meditation. You need and want the most robust set of mind tools at your disposal.

For example, I love a single-pointed focus of awareness. Choosing one point and staying there drops me into deep concentration. But what happens at mile 22 when fatigue makes everything hurt? I can choose one point and do my best to stay there, but when the pinpoint disappears, what do I do?

Having the ability to widen my concentration, leaving my awareness open to whatever flows, allows me to work with anything that arises. That's why it's been helpful to vary my practice and cultivate readiness for what may come.

Summary

These advanced awareness techniques, while difficult to develop, might be the most beneficial tactics to use if your preferred workouts don't have repetitive movements. During a game of a fast-moving sport such as tennis, pickleball, racquetball, basketball, volleyball, or downhill skiing, the ability to remain focused in the moment while the object of meditation rapidly changes will help you excel at your sport while providing an opportunity for insight.

Next, I'll talk about emotions, what they are made of, and how to work with them during your movement meditation.

CHAPTER 7

TANGLES OF EMOTION

How to Meditate on Emotion

How do you deal with emotions that come up in mindful movement practice?

The real question is, "When emotions arise, how do you infuse that experience with awareness and equanimity?" Emotions can be highly charged, painful, and seductive. How then do you work with them?

First, let's look more closely at what emotions actually are.

In one of the earliest Shinzen Young retreats I attended, he explained emotions in such a simple and clear way, I couldn't believe I'd never heard it before. It wasn't in any of the many psychology classes I'd taken, and none of my excellent therapists had discussed this perspective.

Shinzen emphasized that emotions are composed of both thoughts and body sensations.

We use emotion as our object of meditation by observing the arising and passing away of the thoughts and body sensations that comprise that emotion.

He offered a simple analogy.

Think of emotions as a ball of red and white yarn. From a distance, the ball looks pink. But that's not a clear view, because most of us see emotions either from far away or so close up we can't see anything. We push away unpleasant emotions, pull pleasant ones closer, or get swamped to the point of nearly drowning in both. We're not seeing at all.

The mindset skills of intense concentration and equanimity learned in meditation change our perception. On closer examination, the body sensations are red yarn while the thoughts are white. The thoughts and body sensations get tangled so tightly that it creates the illusion of pink.

Plus, the thoughts and body sensations feed off each other. We experience a body sensation, and that leads to a thought. We react to the thought, which leads to more body sensations, which then lead to more thoughts, and on and on in a vicious emotional cycle.

Calm, concentrated practice helps untangle and separate thoughts from body sensations. If we learn to follow the separate threads of body sensations and thoughts, we see each thread arise and pass away. Awareness of their individual processes, especially the fact that they pass, brings freedom. When we learn to let go of the thoughts around a certain emotion and to experience only the bare physical sensation, the emotion will often quietly spend itself, stopping the emotional cycle.

Emotions can be grouped into several broad categories: happy, sad, mad, and afraid. Most emotions fit into more than one category at the same time. Grief? Probably sad and mad. Anger? Clearly mad, but also might be sad and afraid. Joy? Happy, but could be tinged with sad if we miss someone who used to make us happy. Note the flavor of the body sensations and unravel them from the accompanying thoughts to further unlock the grip of a negative emotional state.

The 5 Conditions

During the meditation leader training I took at the Sage Institute for Creativity & Consciousness, they introduced us to "The 5 Conditions," another way to look at the interaction of thoughts and body sensations. Originally set forth by Zen Master Bernie Glassman as an explanation of what Buddhist psychology calls the Skandas, the 5 Conditions were adapted from that source by Sensei Sean Murphy. They provide additional insight into the reality of experience—the truth of what happens in our minds and bodies as we go through life.

The 5 Conditions are:

- Sensation/Perception
- Feeling
- Reaction
- Recognition/Interpretation
- Story

Sensation/Perception

Any experience begins with sensations in the body. Not what you think about the sensation or whether you like it or not, but pure, raw sensation. The touch. The taste. The felt sense. The smell. The sound. The sight. The impact. Sensation is light entering your retina. Nerve endings in the skin of your fingers firing as you grip the steering wheel. Sound entering your ear canal and activating the auditory nerve. It's the taste bud encountering food—that first firing. That's sensation, the first of the five conditions: Pure input into a sense gate. The body's perception of a stimulus entering a sense gate in the present moment—this is as close as we get to the pure experience of reality.

Feeling

Feeling in this case doesn't mean sensations or emotional feeling. It simply means the awareness of whether the sensation is pleasant, unpleasant, or neutral. It's almost instantaneous with the actual sensation. We sense, and then the body registers a quality or flavor of the input as positive (pleasant—I like it), negative (unpleasant—I don't like it), or neutral. For our purposes here, the most important are pleasant and unpleasant.

Reaction

After that comes a reaction. This is where we experience grasping or craving or aversion. This is the way the body pushes and pulls toward or against the experience based on its flavor. You might like or dislike it, find it pleasant or unpleasant. The reaction may be purely internal, or it might be external, such as a physical turning toward or away from the experience. It's also where emotions begin. Fear. Joy. Sadness. Anger. Any of these emotional reactions may occur at this stage. And you may cringe away or lean toward the sensation depending on the flavor of pleasantness or unpleasantness that attends the sensation. A reaction could also be as subtle as the pupils dilating or opening in response to light or dark. These reactions are not yet conscious. They are automatic, survival-based, and evolutionary.

Recognition/Interpretation

Here's where the mind catches up with the three previous processes, which are nearly unconscious. This stage is more conscious. The mind and body realize the stove is hot or the sound loud and shrill. It becomes aware of a sour or bitter taste or the smell of a lovely fragrance. Thoughts may begin to form around it. Words and images in the mind may occur. The concept arises in our mind. We register consciously what has just happened.

Story

Finally, the mind creates a story from the ideas, preconceptions, and memories associated with the situation. For example, "Damn! Who left the stove on!" or "I'm so stupid!" or "Stoves should have safety valves!" Trying to give the event meaning, the mind creates a narrative around it. Often these narratives are false and unhelpful, but not always. Sometimes we do see clearly. Regardless, the story is still four steps removed from that initial sensation. And these four steps can cause a lot of trouble.

Let's say I'm running a race. When I run, I frequently have sensations in my left foot. I don't like them. I react, favor it, and become anxious. I interpret this as a problem. I make up a story. "Oh no! Maybe that surgeon who wanted to fuse my ankle was right. I've probably permanently injured myself. I should stop right now. But if I can't run, I'll gain back all the weight and more. Ed will leave and take the dog." And on and on and on.

The story I made up is plausible. Perhaps I should quit the race, go home, and run another day. But it might not be true. If I had believed one doctor's story about my ankle and taken it on as truth in my own mind, I wouldn't have spent the last decade as a runner and you wouldn't be reading this book. The moral? Don't believe everything you think!

Mindfulness short-circuits this process. Much suffering comes not from the sensation itself, or even the feeling or reaction. It's when we create a story and live as if that story were true that it turns from pure sensation and awareness into suffering.

In this example, rather than follow my train of thought down the rabbit hole, I can catch it quickly and return to observing the pure sensation.

My left foot tingles. End of story.

Mindfulness simplifies our experience into the most basic process.

Mindfulness also offers insight. When we see the process happening and can remain calm and open to it, we see it for what it is, not reality, just a story.

Mindfulness always brings us back to the present moment. The story is usually in the future or the past and is usually fraught. The past is regret or longing for things from before. The future is worry or longing for things to happen a certain way.

So are craving and aversion. We want to push away things from the past when we feel the sensation of regret. And when we worry, we desire to push away things of the future. But we also pull on happy memories of the past, wishing to relive them. We pull on the future, hoping it turns out a certain way.

Thoughts of the future, thoughts of the past, and judgment (especially self-judgment) are full of the potential to create suffering. But a moment-to-moment awareness of the present has no such energy. Pure experience in the moment has no opinion. It's the reaction (that push or pull) or the story that causes suffering. With mindfulness, you see through the layers to what's actually happening. It's a practice in reality.

Any time you take on a new challenge, you will likely notice negative stories arising in the mind—sometimes convincing ones. They offer plausible reasons we can't succeed. People who do succeed see through these negative stories.

Even stories happening in the present can distract. Thoughts of, "I'm no good at this. I'm not cut out for this. I'm not an athlete like [__fill in the blank__]" are stories. Depending on your fitness level, mental ability, and level of training, you might not be cut out for everything you attempt. But please don't let the story keep you from finding out!

Untangling Emotions

The last year my father was alive coincided with my recovery from a major depressive episode during which I had nearly killed myself. He and I spent his final summer playing golf, and he and my mother lived with us in the four months before his death.

As he slowly died and I learned to live again, my meditation practice grew. The experience tested me on multiple levels, primarily emotional.

I wanted nothing more than to spend those days with him on what we fondly referred to as "goat pastures," small courses in rural Licking County, Ohio. But I struggled to keep my mind where my body was. There were so many questions, so many regrets. There was so much confusion about my mental health, my job, my future. And so much sadness that he would soon be gone.

This emotional storm of my father's impending death and my own anxiety and depression presented the most difficult meditation I'd had to date. Unlike the back spasms and sciatic pain that had originally brought me to meditation, I could not escape this.

Each treasured day on the course with him offered rich opportunities to untangle complex emotions. The pure pleasure of being near him intensified as his health dwindled. The layers of these experiences included the agony of seeing this decline, as well as recognizing the up-and-down nature of our relationship through the years, my bad golf game turning good as I watched his award-winning golf game suffer, and the fight against my depression, which caused me to quit my job as a lawyer and kept me in bed nearly every day I wasn't golfing with him.

Pleasant thoughts, unpleasant thoughts; pleasant body sensations, unpleasant body sensations. My new meditation skills were often no match for this tangled flood of emotions.

I didn't yet know about the 5 Conditions, but I knew about creating a story. Along with the grasping of pleasure and pushing away of pain, I noted my

thoughts of how it shouldn't be this way and did my best to let them go. I
untangled the direct sensory, bodily experiences of emotion, separating
them from my thoughts and stories. Pink threads turned to red and white.
Untangling the web of emotions helped me to really be with my father.
And after Dad died, the same techniques helped when hurtling waves of
grief pounded my heart. Practice. Practice. Practice. I'm so grateful I knew
what to do.

Tricky Body

Those of us who live with mental health symptoms may have out-of-
proportion thoughts and body sensations. We might be hypervigilant, with
not just a tricky mind, but a tricky body, too.

When you first begin to meditate and are not used to giving anxiety or
depression such full attention, it might startle you to see how often they
are present. Realizing the temporary nature of the thoughts and body
sensations that make up those conditions can bring relief. When you feel
you can't go on, remember it will change! You've heard the phrase "This too
shall pass." Shinzen reframes that as, "This too IS passing."[24]

In depression, tricky thinking tangles with physical sensations of heaviness
and pain. People think of depression as purely a mind disease, but it
manifests in the body with a leaden, deadened feeling and often a sense of
hopelessness as well, not only in the mind but in the body too. I used to say
it was trying to walk through pudding: Thick and viscous, every move a fight.

Anxiety has a different quality of sensation, more tingling than that of
depression but just as painful. It also often includes unpleasant thoughts,
an extra layer on top of the already unpleasant body sensations. Plus,
hypervigilance often goes with it. People with anxiety may become

---

24 Shinzen Young, "The Power of Gone." November 6, 2015. www.shinzen.org/wp-content/
     uploads/2016/12/art_PowerofGone.pdf.

hyperaware of thoughts and feelings. Anxiety can feel like a vibrational field with electrical zaps, confusion, and waves of adrenaline so powerful the sufferer believes they will knock her down or kill her.

I sat at a retreat where my paranoia, anxiety, and fear were so great and constant that I feared I would collapse. I was grateful that Ed was beside me and Bhante G. at the head of the room. Bhante G. instructed us to let our most powerful thoughts and body sensations become the object of meditation.

I watched thoughts of financial ruin, losing our house, and Ed leaving arise. Strong, painful sensations wracked my chest and belly. I pulled away, then returned. I rode those waves for several sitting periods. It was simultaneously uncomfortable and freeing to know I could sit through that much angst. Until the stillness of the retreat pushed back my world's busy distractions, I hadn't realized how much anxiety and paranoia I'd had inside me. As I sat, any time I let my mind wander, the paranoia returned so strongly I wasn't sure I could keep my seat. But I did, tears streaming down my face.

Then we walked. In the retreat center gymnasium, I plotted a straight line, back and forth across the basketball court. At the end of the line, before I turned, I noticed the desire to turn welling up inside me. But I didn't turn. I stood with that urge, experiencing it, letting it subside, and not turning until it passed and I chose to turn. Only then did I walk back to the other end of the line.

When the next sitting period began, my body felt calmer. The waves of paranoia and anxiety returned, but I knew they would pass. My experience during walking of waiting before I turned, resisting the urge to turn, and just feeling it all the way through transferred over to the sitting. That taste of impermanence from noticing my desire to turn during the walk helped me observe how the waves of emotion, still strong as they were, also rose and fell. And I let them. I can only describe the freedom in that with one word: bliss.

Susan M. Orsillo, PhD, and Lizabeth Roemer, PhD, write about using meditation as an anxiety treatment:

> "We're asking you to notice your anxiety in a new and different
> way. People often hypervigilantly scan for signs of anxiety, either
> to brace for the threats to come or to chastise themselves for
> having an unwanted response. As you monitor your experience,
> try to bring a curious, observing stance to noticing your anxiety.
> The goal is to observe and notice the full range of reactions, not
> to judge or control them. Over time, this new way of relating
> to your anxiety will lead to these signs being less alarming and
> overwhelming."[25]
>
> —Susan M. Orsillo, PhD, and Lizabeth Roemer, PhD

When you experience an emotion all the way through, feel it flow through your body, notice any thoughts that arise with it, and let all of that move and pass away, that's freedom. This level of understanding differs from what we seek in therapy. The insight here is cellular, and it reduces suffering in a powerful way.

Should we meditate through this storm?

It depends!

During times of deep distress, meditation may be difficult regardless of your mental health status. But it also may be the best thing to do. Telling those of us who rely on meditation as a coping tool not to do it is like telling a dancer not to dance with a sore toe, or telling a tennis player to lay off when a knee aches. We take care not to do harm. We don't need to power through. Being a fierce meditation warrior isn't always effective. And we're often not the right one to make that decision. It is such an individual case. Consult a teacher,

---

25 Susan M. Orsillo and Lizabeth Roemer. *The Mindful Way Through Anxiety*, 35.
    mindfulwaythroughanxiety.com.

therapist, or other mentor if you have concerns, especially if you have a history of trauma.

But if you decide to meditate during a tough stretch, the process is the same as with any other object of meditation. Infuse your experience with awareness and equanimity. Isolate the object on which you will focus. Drill into it with your full concentrated awareness while you allow those thoughts and body sensations to be exactly as they are.

YOUR TURN: UNTANGLING EMOTIONS

At first, try this complex exercise while standing or sitting. Once you feel skilled with it, use it during your movement meditation. Choose an interval. Then turn your awareness to an emotionally charged situation, one that arouses strong emotion in you. As you think of it, note where in your body you feel it. Is your throat tight? Does your belly burn? Do tears well up? Spend a few minutes experiencing these body sensations. Then, turn your attention to any thoughts that may also be arising. Do your best to separate the body sensations from the thoughts. Simply note that difference and attempt to let both the thoughts and the body sensations arise, do their little dances, and pass away. Again, this is an advanced practice. It is normal at first to be carried off by either the thoughts or the body sensations. When you remember your intention to meditate, give yourself a little mental cheer, gently bring your mind back to your body, and begin again.

Summary

Now that you know those powerful emotions are simply a tangle of thoughts and body sensations, explore and unravel the threads as you do your movement practice.

The next chapter delves more deeply into how to work with painful and joyous thoughts and body sensations. Grow through movement practice no matter what arises.

CHAPTER 8

HOW TO GROW THROUGH PAIN (AND JOY)

Practicing with Pain and Pleasure

There it was, that familiar twinge. While training for a third marathon, I'd chosen the indoor track over the ice and snow-covered Olentangy Trail. Sixteen miles into the twenty-mile track run, the back spasms began. Time to work with pain.

When Ed introduced me to meditation, I wasn't convinced until I experienced how effectively it addressed pain. In *Depression Hates a Moving Target*, the wonky ankle stole the show. I didn't write about back pain, but mild scoliosis does tweak my back from time to time. The difference is that now I know how to work with it.

Back spasms are just that: spasms. Impermanent. Before I learned to meditate, I tensed during a spasm and steeled myself against the pain. If I'm caught off guard, I still do. But on the track that day, having four more miles to go provided ample opportunity to investigate the spasms. I got curious about them, did my best to relax as each one began, and noticed how they passed.

When my mind yelled at me with the story, "You're ruining your body. You'll be paralyzed! Why didn't you choose a smarter sport?" I made that an object of meditation. All of it coming and going, it was a little theater to watch as I continued to run. Investigating your own back spasms might seem an odd form of entertainment, but it beats being doubled over.

And pain isn't the only teacher. We can also meditate on joy.

With pain, the tendency is to internally push it away. With joy, the tendency is to pull. Skillful practice requires us to neither push nor pull, regardless of the experience. As counterintuitive as it sounds, we learn to turn toward pain, release joy, and notice what happens. Then, we recycle any response into the practice.

Pleasure, like any other experience, is made up of thoughts and body sensations. In your movement practice, you have the option to choose pleasant thoughts, pleasant body sensations, or both to serve as the object of meditation. Relax into them. Notice what happens when you do. The inner grasping for more pleasure actually diminishes pleasure. Often, when you pay close attention to pleasant experiences and do so with a balanced mind, the pleasure increases. You may have the urge to cling to that increased pleasure. Notice that. Turn your attention to whatever happens.

Shinzen offered this splendid equation about pain and suffering:

Suffering equals pain multiplied by resistance.[26]

If your pain is a 7 out of 10 and you resist at a level of 6 out of 10, you suffer around a level of 42 out of 100. If instead you open to the pain and infuse it

---

26   Shinzen Young, "Natural Pain Relief." (December 7, 2016). www.shinzen.org/wp-content/uploads/2016/12/art_synopsis-pain.pdf.

with equanimity, the suffering drops. You might not be able to lower how you resist to level 1, but even at a level 3, your suffering will only be a 21 instead of a 42.

While I don't know Shinzen's exact formula for joy, the same principle works. Joy experienced in the present moment without craving is bliss. Infusing joy with equanimity by not interfering with the thoughts and body sensations around it makes it last longer and be more fulfilling. Grasping after joy ruins it.

The Power of Pain

Pain often pulls at us more intensely than the breath or other body sensations. Rather than trying to ignore it and hold fiercely to a different object of meditation, we might have a more fruitful meditation session if we tune into that pain.

The peril here is trying to train the mind to focus where you set it. If you want to train that puppy mind to sit and stay, but you tell it to sit, then ignore it when it walks out of the room, you have only trained yourself in the art of aggravation. The puppy knows your intention is meaningless. In meditation, exert gently. Train the mind to return to the place you put it with a firm nudge, not a slap or a smack.

Ways to Focus on Pain

Different types of awareness work better with different types of pain.

When I have a minor injury that produces a sharp pain, I focus on that painful spot with a single focus that is one-dimensional in width, but infinite in depth. For example, a few months ago, I cut one of my toenails too short. I took a few days off from running to make sure the wound healed. Then, I bandaged it and went on a run. Even though I wasn't damaging the toe further, every once in a while, the toe sent out a little jolt. That ouch would have been easy to ignore, but I chose that as my object of meditation.

I noted the sharpness and heat, not thinking about it, but letting my consciousness soak deeply into that experience. This might sound masochistic, but it was the perfect object of meditation. Because pain grabs your attention, it doesn't require much effort to hold your focus.

By relaxing around this unpleasant sensation, I was able to continue running and even feel a fondness for my poor toe I had unintentionally maimed.

That single point of pain focused my mind. I noted it arising and passing. This allowed me to maintain my running form, not limp, and avoid injuring another part of my body by favoring that toe.

Broader or free-floating awareness works better with the dull ache or overall body pain of fatigued muscles as well as the mental fatigue that comes with endurance sports. Experiment with different types of focus. It keeps the practice fresh and helps you take control of your meditation experience. Dive deep into it with curiosity. Open up to whatever changes might occur in the pain place. Let those changes become your guide.

But please do not exercise if it will cause damage. While a minor injury may be an inconvenience and an opportunity, pain can also signal a time to rest or see a medical professional. Take care of yourself and live to practice mindful movement another day.

Desensitizing Around Painful Sounds

I use meditation to overcome difficulties around unpleasant thoughts and body sensations, specifically leaf blower and lawn mower sounds. If a landscape crew was on our street, I used to feel panicked, as if the machines (not the workers) might attack, even though I knew I was perfectly safe. My mind filled with images of drowning in the sound. Negative and judgmental thoughts arose: "Stupid leaf blowers. Why do they have to be so loud?" I could remind myself all day of my safety, but my jaw tightened, my throat closed, and my stomach tensed regardless. When I first began to run, I took the "wrong" medicine. If I saw a landscape company vehicle on our street, I waited until they left.

Eventually, I had enough of this phobia and used meditation to desensitize myself. I began by running to the end of our short street then back to the house while a landscape vehicle was there, using the unpleasant body sensations relating to the sounds as my object of meditation.

I started with a narrow focus of attention, turning the mind camera onto one particular sensation in my body: usually agitation, which feels like a tense vibration in my face and chest. After I'd passed a few houses, I opened my awareness to the thoughts filling my mind: "Why are these things so loud!" and "I have to get out of here!"

At first, I had no equanimity and no awareness that the sensations and thoughts moved. But leaf blowers continued to offer an opportunity to untangle thoughts from body sensations and a chance to drop the scary story I had made. I built up to longer intervals, used a wider focus of awareness, and kept doing my best to open my mind and calm myself. Eventually, I was able to leave the house for a run even if a landscaping truck was on the street.

Leaf blowers and lawnmowers still demand my attention. But I have choices. I can be pissed off about how these sounds ruin my peaceful, meditative run. I can ignore them and push myself to focus on my breath or other sensations, or I can broaden my awareness, work with what's arising, and let the leaf blowers and lawnmowers—and my illusions about them—be the object. It still requires effort. I'll never enjoy the sounds. But they no longer trap me in the house. That progress generates positive body sensations, and I focus on those.

The Pain of Mental Health Challenges

During my first big race, the Capital City Half and Quarter Marathon in Columbus, my anxiety nearly kept me from even signing up. On race day, when we hadn't allowed enough time to arrive and park, my body flooded with unpleasant jolts of adrenaline. It felt as if my head was going to come off, and I was certain my heart would explode from the pounding.

Depression, anxiety, mania, and other mental health issues have specific qualities of pain, primarily mental and emotional—although depression has a heaviness, and anxiety and mania have an agitation, both of which are quite physical.

Meditation can desensitize these. Tiny doses of exposure (my leaf blower desensitization) can allow you to turn these experiences into tools for insight. By focusing directly on the place in the body where the anxiety arises and following the thoughts that come and go with an anxiety outbreak, you will see the impermanence within it and learn that it will not harm you.

At that race, as my friend Leslee and I approached the starting corrals and I saw the throng of people pushed together in the small spaces, my head began to swim. I stopped, unable to walk any further.

"I need to go to the bathroom," I said and joined a long line at the bank of port-o-potties by the start corrals.

When I emerged from the plastic box, Leslee said, "Let's just stand at the corral entrance. Once everyone starts to move, then we'll jump in."

I heaved a sigh of relief. My anxiety didn't disappear, but I knew what to do.

We walked to the opening and stood next to it, letting others pass through as we waited. As we stood, I did a quick scan: tremble in my arms, shuddering in my belly, pounding in my heart. I found the sensation that was most prominent, my rasping breath, and poured all of my awareness into it. Even within the shortness of my breathing, I found the familiar in breath, the turn, the out breath, and the splendid quiet pause. I sank my awareness into the pause, staying with it until my body naturally pulled breath in again.

When the clamor of the crowd of excited runners and walkers eager to start broke my concentration, I gently returned my focus to my breath. In, turn, out, pause. In, turn, out, pause. Old faithful. Right here. Safe and secure in this moment.

Other body sensations shouted for attention. Now that I had relaxed into the breath, I scanned those again, giving each one a hit of awareness before shifting to the safety of the breath, which had deepened and calmed.

The crowd began to move. Our turn came, and Leslee asked, "Ready?" I had a choice. I could hop in and go or miss this chance. I nodded and stepped through the opening. My first big race had begun.

Anxiety and Panic

Another word about anxiety and panic. When I first began to experience anxiety, especially panic attacks, I could not meditate directly on the experience. First, I had to convince myself that I would not die from the panic attack. Panic attack symptoms mimic a heart attack. So, I went to the emergency room not once, not twice, not three times, but more times than I can remember. Each time, kind medical professionals checked me thoroughly and told me I did not have any heart problems but was probably suffering from anxiety.

If we encounter an experience in which the thoughts and body sensations come so fast that they override our skill at separating them, we probably can't meditate through that. Shinzen calls this "freak out."[27]

When I first heard him use that expression, I knew that was what happened when I had extreme anxiety that turned into panic. Even after years of meditation, my ability to focus and maintain equanimity was no match for the virtual flood of thoughts and sensations. Meditating on extreme anxiety and panic is PhD level stuff. Trauma-informed practitioners offer techniques that combine meditation with other practices. It's a bit like dipping your toe into meditation and then taking it out, titrating the dose, so to speak, in order to prevent freak-out. It is beyond the scope of this book, but I have mentioned it in the Resources section in the back of this book.

To stave off freak-out (although I doubt they would call it that), a mental health professional might suggest anti-anxiety medications. I choose not to take anything addictive. I have no opinion on what you should do. That's between you and your doctor. If you have addiction issues, be aware of that and do what you need.

Not having medication to shield me from the symptoms forced me to deal with panic head-on. But first, I had to become convinced a panic attack *would not kill me*. Yes, I felt like I was dying. My mind screamed, "You are going to die!" I also feared I would pass out, but I did not. I used meditation to get through.

With the right effort, most people can build the focus and equanimity necessary to tease out the thoughts and body sensations and limit the suffering around anxiety. But to be willing to do so, you have to be done. *Really, really done*. And you probably will have had to try many other things first. Again, no judgment. Just know I'm cheering you on regardless of what you choose.

---

27   Shinzen Young, "Shinzen Young: The Science of Enlightenment, Part 1." Sounds True. Accessed November, 2021. resources.soundstrue.com/transcript/shinzen-young-the-science-of-enlightenment-part-1.

Depression

With my depression, heaviness of body, sluggish mind, and defeatist thoughts become my objects of meditation. Walking the dog in what felt like slow motion, I noticed how the thoughts arose and passed away. "This will never end." And "If I were a better person, I could just push through." And "Why is this happening to me?"

I did not try to push these thoughts away, reframe them, or even question them. Instead, I noticed. I let them arise, talk, and pass away. Often, by the end of our walk, they dissipated. Other days, they remained. But I did not get caught in them. Meditation while walking reduced the suffering they caused.

This is another example of separating the yarns of emotion. Untangling threads of thought and body sensation while maintaining a calm mental state reduces the suffering around the symptoms of mental health challenges.

Motivation

Tiny Goals

Anyone else have trouble getting yourself moving? No need to raise your hand. We know and understand.

Running dug me out of a horrible depression. It soothes my anxiety. I've been able to reduce my antidepressants. But even now, despite having run more than 12,000 miles, I can still have trouble getting started.

One of my remedies is to choose a goal so small, it's impossible for me to fail.

I tell myself I'm just going to run around the block. Once I get going, I usually go more.

If agoraphobia flares and I can't force myself to leave the house, house jogging (literally jogging around our ranch-style house) counts.

Or a few laps up and down the hallway might be the best I can do.

You know what doesn't help? Adding a guilt and shame story. I do what I can and count that as a win.

Notice Thoughts Around Movement

I used to *exercise* primarily to lose weight. Now, I *move* to improve my mood. I enjoy that movement helps me maintain a healthy weight, but finding a form that brings me joy shifted the energy around it. It's a celebration of this amazing thing we call a "body."

Notice your thoughts around movement. Does a story you've created or an unpleasant body sensation keep you from trying? Does moving seem like it might be difficult, boring, or dull? Simply notice.

Bad Weather

When I was younger, I detested winter. I even hated fall because it led to the inevitable winter. I'm still not a huge fan, but mindful movement transformed my attitude.

Back in December, when it snowed, I took the pupperina for a short jog/walk with the emphasis on walk to avoid sliding on ice. We looked at holiday lights and had a fabulous encounter with the "forest doggos" (a.k.a., deer).

I still don't bounce out the door if it's cold or rainy. It may take hours of circling the hall tree before I pull on boots, gloves, hat, and all the layers needed to stay warm. But once I get going, it's glorious.

Here's the trick: Stay in the moment. When I'm putting on my boots, I'm just putting on my boots. I notice thoughts of dread and bring my mind back to my boots. That helps me get out the door.

How to Make Yourself Move

When motivation wanes, I can't always make myself move. I try and rebel. That's my nature. It helps to know yourself. Working with your natural tendencies is more successful than fighting them.

This reminds me of Zen work at retreats. Ed first studied meditation at Zen Mountain Monastery with Zen Master John Daido Loori. Ed's first work assignment was kitchen duty. He found that chopping vegetables and making food brought him joy. As soon as Zen Master John Daido Loori discovered how much Ed loved it, they reassigned him. The idea was that it needed to be a challenge. Maybe Daido thought Ed was taking the wrong medicine, that Ed needed to experience pain as well as joy. Perhaps your resistance is the inquiry. Perhaps you need to push yourself in order to grow.

You might need a group, which meditators call the "Sangha."

You might need a challenge. Adapt a traditional meditation challenge to include movement or transform a movement challenge by adding meditation.

Perhaps competition suits you. Find someone and strike a bet or make a dare.

The key is to find what motivates you. Nature? Your dog? Fellowship? Responsibility? Service to others? Achievement? Competition? Input? Find that and do that. Another running joke: "Would I jump off a cliff? I don't know. Is there a medal?"

If you continue to resist, recycle that reaction. Resistance thoughts and body sensations are yet another quality of pain. Make that your object. Chunk them down. Notice every step. Slowly feel your way through it all. The best way to know yourself is to see those thoughts as they arise, do their little dance, and pass away. One of the best ways to know yourself is to meditate.

Cheerleader and Critic

I've been training hard, running, and walking a lot of miles. My body hurts and my mind reels.

A mean coach inside me yells that I was stupid to sign up for the race I'm training for. It also says I'm lazy for not being able to go faster. It jeers, saying other people are doing better.

But beside the mean coach, a cheerleader bounces up and down. She's got pom poms and a megaphone. It's hard to hear her over the meanie. But the more I listen, the louder she gets. She tells me I'm doing great, listening to my body, and taking care of what I need so I can live to move another day.

Most of us have these two parts and more. Mindful meditation practice includes noticing those voices, sensing the thoughts they offer, and letting them arise, move, and pass away. If you struggle getting into your movement, let that cheerleader and those pom poms motivate you. Once you have a solid movement meditation practice, try to notice both and let them pass.

Joy

What about joy? You promised us joy!

I did! And guess what! You already know how to meditate on joy, happiness, splendor, ecstasy, and all the pleasant feels.

Repeat after me: *Infuse your experience with awareness and equanimity!*

Let's go back to my first big race, the Capital City Half Marathon, the one that took all my meditation skills to even begin. Once I crossed that start line, anxiety and near panic transformed into a deep satisfaction, one which at times morphed into bliss.

That starting-line freak-out sharpened my attention and heightened my awareness. A flood of pleasant sensations swept away the unpleasant ones. Those initial thoughts of "I'm going to pass out" became "I'm running a *huge* race!" and "I'm not going to be last." When pleasant thoughts and sensations arose, I experienced them as fully as I could, then let them go, opening to whatever happened in real time.

Occasionally, neutral sensations and thoughts like, "Are we done yet?" arose. Concentration and equanimity built from years of practice allowed me to stay with boredom and blankness and not push them away. The race turned into a carnival of thoughts and sensations, mostly pleasant or neutral, which caused more pleasant thoughts and sensations to arise.

The smile on my face as I crossed that finish line radiated through my body. No need to grab at the emotion or hold it. Allowing it to do its dance was more than enough pleasure. When the feeling passed, I let it go.

Summary

I can never hear it often enough myself, so I'll repeat it now. You have the option to meditate on any experience, including pain and joy. The formula is always the same: Infuse your experience (thoughts and body sensations) with awareness and equanimity. Whatever arises as a result of that pain or joy can become part of your practice. Recycle. Recycle. Recycle.

Next, I'll talk more about the mind states and offer a framework to help you think about them more clearly. You'll see how meditation helps develop useful mind states, another part of the path toward reducing suffering.

CHAPTER 9

CULTIVATING MIND STATES

The Mind States

The Buddhist tradition mentions four mind states to cultivate:

- Equanimity
- Compassion
- Empathetic joy
- Loving-kindness

The teaching of these mind states predates the Buddha, having originated with Hinduism, but they have been widely adopted in Buddhist teachings.[28]

When I first began to practice, I had a misconception about developing mind states. I thought I was supposed to let everything go. I did not realize I could use that "right effort" to turn my mind toward helpful things. It seemed too close to the "Fake it 'til you make it," "Create your reality," or "Think it and it shall be so," mindset I had followed to my detriment earlier in life.

---

28 "Brahmavihara." Accessed November, 2021. en.wikipedia.org/wiki/Brahmavihara.

At one retreat, I even challenged Bhante G.

"Isn't this just fake positivity?" I asked.

He smiled, thanked me for my question, and reminded me that we do not force mind states to happen. We set an intention to notice them and enjoy them when they arise.

Equanimity

Let's look again at the equanimity so essential to our mindful movement practice. I can hear Natalie Goldberg saying, "Let the whole world come home to you." Receive the experience as it comes, accepting it as it is. She said that quietly while we did slow walking practice, suggesting we feel the bottoms of our feet as we walked, being only in the step we were taking, not ahead or behind.

Equanimity is freedom. We let our experience, those sensations in our splendid body, and those thoughts in our tricky minds happen naturally and without interference. While equanimity is categorized as a "mind state," it might also be considered a heart or body state. It flows through everything. You do your best to adopt it. See what I did? "Do your best." So equanimous.

Compassion and Empathetic Joy

One of the most powerful insights that can occur in our movement meditation is the awareness of the plight of others. Compassion, the desire that others be free from suffering, arises as we experience our own freedom. It may stir you to want to tell others about meditation, or you may wish to lead by example, simply being your best self in all areas of your life.

Empathetic joy rises from insight as well. When we see that we are not separate from others, it becomes easier to want the best for everyone. We celebrate the successes of others and take pleasure in their joys.

Work with compassion and empathetic joy by noticing when they arise naturally and allowing the mind to linger on them, examining what they are made of. (Hint: The ingredients are particular qualities of thoughts and body sensations.) Some teachers may ask you to foster these states, to imagine yourself feeling them. If you can do this, fine. But if you feel any resistance, go back to the natural state of attending to your actual experience in the moment while remaining in equanimity.

We tend to forget about self-compassion. Especially in elite sports, but even in everyday fitness circles, compassion doesn't sound tough enough. In reality, being tender with yourself on the inside, even as you do a challenging workout, helps foster inner strength. You won't be tossed away when things get difficult if you've learned how to be respectful and gentle with yourself. It's another aspect of not fighting yourself. You're not being soft; you're being kind.

Loving-Kindness (Metta)

Metta, also known as loving-kindness, is a mental attitude developed and maintained through practice. Metta meditation practice is scientifically proven to increase kindness and positivity toward others and improve feelings of social connection.[29]

Contrary to popular opinion, Metta is not about being nice, although that benefit may happen. Metta also does not require sentimentality or affection. Rather, Metta practice creates conditions that allow the quality of loving-kindness to arise naturally within us.

To practice, we repeat a series of phrases aloud or to ourselves. We start by thinking of someone for whom we have genuine affection since we already have Metta naturally for that person. It's easy to notice our thoughts

---

29   Seppala, Emma PhD. "18 Science-Backed Reasons to Try Loving-Kindness Meditation" *Psychology Today*, September 15, 2014. www.psychologytoday.com/us/blog/feeling-it/201409/18-science-backed-reasons-try-loving-kindness-meditation.

and body sensations of loving-kindness for that individual. That helps us identify the experience of loving-kindness.

Then, we repeat the phrases while thinking of different people: someone more neutral, a difficult person, ourselves, and finally, everyone. Bringing to mind people with whom we have these varied types of relationships strengthens our Metta muscle. We see how far Metta can reach.

Unlike the prayer practices of other traditions such as Christianity, in Metta practice, we do not petition an outside entity. The Metta generated through this practice comes from our experience (i.e., our thoughts and body sensations).

We also don't need to pretend to like the phrases or force ourselves to think kind thoughts when that's not what's in our hearts and minds. Again, we simply create conditions to allow loving-kindness to arise, and notice when it does.

YOUR TURN: METTA

To practice Metta, repeat phrases while you bring to mind certain individuals. The phrases used in Metta practice are a type of mantra. Make the phrases and any thoughts and body sensations that arise your object of meditation.

Here are some typical phrases:

> May you be well.
>
> May you be peaceful.
>
> May you be happy.
>
> May no harm come to you.
>
> May you be free from suffering.
>
> May you live with comfort and ease.

Start by bringing to mind a person or being (who could be a pet) for whom you have unconditional positive regard. Choose someone with whom you have no conflict whatsoever. When you have them in mind, repeat those phrases.

Next, think of a person you adore. This could be your partner, spouse, or parent. It might be a child. When you have them in mind, repeat those phrases.

Next, bring to mind a neutral person. This could be a store clerk or the bus driver or someone you see regularly, but for whom you have no strong feelings. When you have them in mind, repeat those phrases.

Then, bring to mind a difficult person. When you have them in mind, repeat those phrases.

Next, bring yourself to mind. Repeat those phrases directed toward yourself using "I."

Finally, think of the whole world with all the people you love, the ones you don't know, the difficult ones, and the ones you adore. When you have them in mind, repeat the phrases using the words "we" and "us" instead of "you."

Feel free to create your own phrases as I sometimes do.

After a particularly disturbing political event, as I ran through our neighborhood, I noticed how the sight of political banners and flags for politicians who oppose my views brought me physical pain. My mind filled with unkind thoughts. I was harboring ill will toward the neighbors in those houses, most of whom I barely knew.

I decided to try Metta.

Going by the house of a neighbor-friend, under my breath I chanted, "May you be well. May you be happy. May no harm come to you. May you be free from greed, hatred, and delusion." I added this final phrase because it felt appropriate.

Next, I ran past several houses of people I do not know, but who had no flags or banners. Again, I chanted "May you be well. May you be happy. May no harm come to you. May you be free from greed, hatred, and delusion."

As I approached a house with an "offending" flag, I began the Metta phrases again. I noticed my gritted teeth and clenched fists. I opened my hands, relaxed my jaw, and whispered, "May you be well. May you be happy. May no harm come to you. May you be free from greed, hatred, and delusion."

After I was well past that house, I extended the Metta to all, including me and my anger. I chanted out loud, "May WE be well. May we be happy. May no harm come to us. May we be free from greed, hatred, and delusion."

As the words escaped my lips, I relaxed. I did not want to hate my neighbors. In fact, I didn't even know them. I only knew I was afraid and that I wished for us all to be well, happy, and free. A tear froze on my cheek. I wiped it and continued to run.

Practice

We practice our sport. We practice meditation. We practice showing up for life.

What's so special about the word "practice"?

Transformation happens through practice. Meditation practice, specifically, changes you on a cellular level: not just your brain, but your mind—the whole of you.

For someone like me—highly competitive one day, and frozen by anxiety the next—making movement a *practice* dissolves perfectionism, reduces the strain, and makes it more enjoyable. We will never be perfect. We don't need to be. We only need to continue.

Despite what some motivational speakers insist, we cannot give 100 percent every day. In an interview, Olympic marathon record-holder Eliud Kipchoge explained that he only goes all out on race day. During the rest of his many hours of training, he holds something back. He is practicing.

Even on race day, game day, the day of your show, contest, or performance, you are still practicing. You are just practicing all out, at the highest level of your ability.

In meditation, you practice noticing. You practice being in the body and the mind. And you will be swept away—you will have preferences and crave pleasant experiences. You might try to recreate a lovely walk, a fast race time, a strong climb, a thrilling dance, or your most powerful serve return. This will happen whether you meditate while sitting, standing, lying down, or moving.

Practice allows you to show up on the splendid days as well as the days when the trail feels like (or actually is) mud. It lets you recover when you fail to summit the mountain, when your free throw is off, and when you're sure there's a hole in your racquet.

Practice helps us find peace, if not joy, regardless of what happens in the body and mind. We may try to win the race, but we try to win (or lose) without suffering. It's holistic. In the ChiRunning system, they suggest "gradual progress." We are a work in progress, practicing to the end.

Acceptance vs. Resignation

One unfair criticism Buddhism receives is that it creates passive people. Some people worry that this level of acceptance will turn them into a doormat. But this is not true. Leaders of certain Buddhist sects devote themselves to activism—the late Thich Nhat Hanh, the Dalai Lama, Bernie Glassman, Joan Halifax, and Pema Chodron, to name a few.

Becoming open and aware to your experience will not turn you into a doormat. Just the opposite. When you don't fight with yourself on the inside, your efforts on the outside become less effortful. When you let go of trying to control your experience of the world, you have less tension. This frees energy, allowing you to put more effort in the right places—the *right effort*.

You are not resigned or defeated. You are a warrior, using your energy effectively, with the flow, not against it. Equanimity helps the energy go the way it wants to. You learn to shape that flow, nudging it. Directing it gently. Not pushing the rope. Not pushing the river.

Another ChiRunning principle is to make sure all the parts of your body move in the direction you want to go. Eyes forward. Feet forward. Body falls forward. Arms swing forward. Knees forward. Nothing to interrupt the flow. This is a physical manifestation of equanimity. Developing this attitude during movement practice helps us achieve it in the rest of our lives.

Don't Know Mind

The mind loves to know things. It craves making meaning. Muddled and confused thinking may generate unpleasant body sensations. Similarly, when you find an answer or solve a puzzle, pleasant body sensations arise.

"Don't know mind" is an aspect of equanimity. Becoming familiar and comfortable with not knowing, we open the mind to what is: reality.

Work with this in movement meditation. Recently, I had a bout of norovirus. The worst of it lasted three or four days, but I still spiked a fever every few days after and fatigue lingered. When I finally got out to walk the pupperina, I turned this into my object of meditation.

As we walked, I noticed the air and the colors. I'd been in the house for ten days. A neighbor had painted their house. My mind wavered, deciding whether it liked the new look or not. I noted my judgment, "I like it," and felt the welling of pleasant body sensations.

But I felt fatigued. We hadn't even reached the end of our quarter-mile long street. "When will I be well enough to run?" and "When will I be well enough to write?" arose.

I noticed the physical discomfort this confusion created—a kind of ache and sadness in my face and belly. That generated more thoughts, a spiral of questions. "Is it something serious?" and "Will I even be able to walk my next race?" and "What if I can't meet my writing deadline?"

My body felt tight and heavy, repelling the confusion and the drag on my mood. I turned that reaction into my object. I consciously relaxed my belly, let my shoulders drop, and kept walking. I didn't fight, change, or push on the experience. Instead, I got curious. Where did I feel the sensations? Did the thoughts have a shape? What happened if I didn't fight them, but just let them do their thing?

Most importantly, I didn't feed the thoughts.

When the rush of thoughts began to spiral faster than I could stay present to them, I brought my awareness back to my feet and let the thoughts float by. I felt my feet in my shoes, the shifting of my weight, the way the air felt on my skin.

That's how I infuse experience with equanimity: relaxing inwardly, an internal acceptance of reality, an inner gentleness. Because of my diminished physical state, I cut the walk short.

But in that exertion, I stayed calm inside. I observed the thoughts. I felt the sadness at not knowing. I observed the texture of thoughts as they arose, danced, and passed away. I observed what "don't know" felt like. When I got home, I went back to bed.

Vows

As part of my practice, I took the following Buddhist vows, called "precepts":

- Refrain from taking life. Not killing any living being.

- Refrain from taking what is not given. Not stealing from anyone.

- Refrain from the misuse of the senses. Not having too much sensual pleasure.

- Refrain from wrong speech.

- Refrain from intoxicants that cloud the mind.

When Shinzen offered the vows to anyone interested, he made it clear that no one needed to take vows. No one needs to do anything to meditate, except meditate. The purpose of taking vows is to make a public statement that you are embarking on the meditative path and will do your best to keep these vows. An inner part of you believes it. It's a tradition. By taking vows with Shinzen, it showed I intended to study with him.

The vows apply to much more than meditation. I see parallels in many areas, including movement meditation.

First, no killing. Ed and I failed at being vegan or vegetarian. So, we limit the amount of meat we eat. Technically, since neither of us kill any of the animals or fish, we're not violating the vow. But that always seems a bit shaky. I keep this in mind when trying any food plan that suggests an abundance of meat. And when I desire a good steak, I notice. And yes, I'm one of those types who puts a cup over wasps and spiders to transport them to the outdoors.

Second, refrain from taking what is not given. Of course, don't steal your friend's unicorn running hat, but this vow is broader than that. When I first began running, I used to pick up interesting things I found on my run: children's toys, a dime-store ring, baubles, and once even a twenty-dollar bill. Now, I might pocket the money, but I take a photo of the items instead.

Someone might come back for them. Plus, it's interesting to notice my desire for these baubles.

Third, avoiding too much sensual pleasure. Gratefully, I've been happily involved with Ed the entire time I've been meditating. He was, after all, my first teacher. But sensual pleasure comes in many forms, including crazy expensive races, gear, and clothes. Because of my bipolar disorder, I try not to get too revved. It can set me up for a crash. I've fallen down rabbit holes with this. I am grateful that meditation helps me to see this coming. When I slide off track, equanimity brings me back to center.

Fourth, being careful with my words. I'd like to think I am more cheerleader than gossip, but I know that's not always the case. Locker room talk can go downhill quickly. And what do I say about myself? This vow helps me remember that what I say about myself and others has power. I fail. I remember. I regroup.

Finally, refraining from intoxicants. As a recovering person, I don't drink alcohol or use drugs, but caffeine and sugar can also create harm. This is another growth opportunity for me.

The vows remind me to practice and bring me back to helpful mind states. When things in movement meditation or life are off, I look at the vows for a possible solution.

Mind Health

While meditation does not promise mental stability, these helpful mind states offer insight into the mind-body process. That expanded understanding can relieve symptoms and facilitate mental health treatment just in itself.

Equanimity, for example, balances the mind. A form of acceptance, equanimity allows a person to see clearly what is happening. It may help you realize when you need a therapist. It might prompt you to try medication or change a medication that's no longer working. And it may reduce hypervigilance and help you avoid a full-blown panic attack.

That same balance of mind may prompt you to shift gears in your workout regimen if things get tough or you tire of a rigid schedule. It also helps you know when to kick things up a notch, firing more of those neurotransmitter switches that make exercise feel good in the first place. Plus, the energy you gain when you stop fighting with yourself boosts both your mood and your performance.

Compassion bolsters mental health. A compassionate heart is both a physical and an emotional ballast against the pain life can bring. Caring about others helps you take positive action for yourself and others.

Compassion's corollary, self-compassion, transforms that inner critic (once you see and hear it for what it is) into an inner cheerleader. We cannot care for ourselves (or others) without compassion for ourselves. Remember the old adage, "Put your own oxygen mask on first"? It's no truer anywhere than with our mental health and well-being. You cannot heal by beating up on yourself, despite what some coaches, trainers, or even a few therapists say. Pain does not equal gain.

Empathetic joy makes you a good friend to others in your workout community, as well as the rest of your life. It's not forced. You will naturally want the best for everyone when this mind state is developed. The resulting sense of community and connectedness combats loneliness and depression. It also helps you serve as a good example to others, and there's not much less depressing than that.

And finally, loving-kindness lifts moods by generating all kinds of happy neurotransmitters. Those happy transmitters may not cure mental health conditions, but they sure are wonderful to have around.

The mind states serve as antidotes to many mental health symptoms, another powerful benefit you will derive from movement practice.

Summary

Movement meditation is a bit like an experiment in a controlled environment. We create conditions that help certain things happen, including an unforced, naturally positive change in the way we think and feel. Cultivating loving-kindness, compassion, empathetic joy, and equanimity helps not only with our practice, but in the rest of our lives.

Next, I'll talk about unhelpful mental habits. These may occur in life or in your movement meditation and can be used if you get stuck to figure out what might need a tweak.

CHAPTER 10

STRUGGLING? CHECK THE HINDRANCES

5 Hindrances Defined

As the name suggests, the hindrances are mental factors that may hinder progress in movement, meditation, and life. They block concentration, tranquility, and mindfulness. Think of the five hindrances as a checklist to help you find what aspect needs attention and what approach to take to solve it.

These are the five hindrances:

- **Clinging or Grasping** (often referred to as sensory desire): seeking pleasure through the five senses of sight, sound, smell, taste, and physical feeling.
- **Ill Will**: feelings of hostility, resentment, hatred, and bitterness.
- **Sloth and Torpor**: half-hearted action with little or no concentration.
- **Restlessness and Worry**: the inability to calm the mind.
- **Doubt**: lack of conviction or trust.

I suffer from them all.

Clinging and grasping arises when I crave a particular experience. If I've had joy in running, I naturally want that again. But grasping gets in the way of experiencing the actual joy available in the moment because I'm focused on a joy I had in the past or might get in the future. Overcoming this hindrance requires equanimity. I must let go of the grasp I have on the thing I want. It also requires concentration to bring me back to the present moment.

Remember that run when I was mad at the neighbors who don't share my political beliefs? Ill will is a polite way of saying how I felt. I did Metta (loving-kindness), but also turned the resentful body sensations into the objects of meditation and noticed my heart softening.

When I feel anxious, restlessness and worry become my companions. Mine are often financial fears or a fear of being disgraced. Despite all the miles (and races) I've run, I still worry about not finishing, getting lost, or looking foolish. Any part of practice that brings me back into the present helps. I often use the visual field, especially colors, because of their power to capture my mind.

When I'm depressed, I experience sloth and torpor, but not for lack of trying. My mind simply won't focus. It's like sludge in my brain. On days when I don't feel like running, I do my best to be gentle with myself, since depression often is the cause. Sleepiness and lack of focus can also be resistance. When that is the case, I bring my mind back to a sharp, one-pointed focus such as the breath or a single body sensation. Again, vision is the easiest for me. I choose a color, often green in summer or gray in winter, and notice when I see it. That bit of right effort helps me focus and brings energy.

Doubt used to rule my life. Now, I turn the thoughts and body sensations around doubt into objects of meditation. But the act of showing up to my movement meditation, day after day, during training and on race days, despite fear, also dispels doubt. I wrote at length about this doubt in *Depression Hates a Moving Target*. I continued to worry I wasn't a real runner regardless of the distances I ran. But the effort of doing what was in front of me, day after day, in the face of doubt and other hindrances, showed me what was true. Attending to reality changed me.

When you find the hindrance that's your sticking point, make the thoughts and body sensations that hindrance creates into your object of meditation. Cultivate the mind state that counters it. Despite years of meditation, I still experience hindrances. Once I am aware of one, it becomes part of the practice.

Music as Motivation

I often hear people say they can't work out without listening to music. If your movement form requires music, that's not an issue. You can dance or do Zumba, aerobics, and Nia without it, but where's the fun?

But what if my fitness routine doesn't require music? Should I listen to music or not?

You already know I'm going to say, "It depends."

Look at your motive. If the music isn't necessary for your movement routine, is it an escape? Can you infuse your experience (the sound of the music) with awareness and equanimity? Only you know the answer. Are you actually meditating? Or have sloth and torpor come calling?

When I run outdoors, I don't listen to music even with bone conduction headphones. Having nearly been hit by vehicles many times, I want to be fully aware of my surroundings. Plus, I use the sounds of nature (as well as leaf blowers) as objects of meditation.

This doesn't mean you must skip the music. Just be honest with yourself. Are you meditating? It's fine regardless.

Just please, be safe. *Always*. As far as we know, you can't reap the physical benefits of meditation (or achieve enlightenment) if you are dead. Please stay alive.

If you can safely use music in your workout and you've developed enough meditation skills, use music as your object. Sound sensations in your body or thoughts in your mind are all grist for the mill. And you knew I was going to say that.

Hindrances and Mental Health

Those of us with mental health challenges may experience more severe hindrances, but that doesn't mean we can't meditate. Although running greatly improved my mental health, the hindrances remain. During a depressive episode, my work on any given run becomes acceptance of sloth and torpor with gentle pushing back. I feel that lead in my arms and the heavy thoughts, and I invite them to run with me.

Before running helped me reduce the number of medications I took, the drugs that saved me also made it difficult to concentrate. Some runs became a study in lack of focus. Other days, resentment at having a debilitating mental health condition turned my mind into a seething cauldron. I meditated using that.

My desire to be better, and even for meditation to magically make me better, still gets in the way. Why am I not faster? Why can't I run farther? And always, doubt, my constant companion, rises again and again. These too are fodder for practice. I'll never run out of things to which to turn my attention.

Each one is a new opportunity, a new chance to shine the light of awareness onto what is happening in any given moment, to experience the process from the inside, and to watch my body and mind do their thing.

Equanimity and self-compassion help. Gentle. Gentle. Gentle. Also, persistence. And support from a teacher and a community. I'll talk more about those last two soon.

Summary

When we struggle with meditation, the five hindrances: sensory desire, ill will, sloth and torpor, restlessness and worry, and doubt, provide clues for changes we might make. Notice where any of the hindrances create difficulty in your practice or life. Awareness alone can bring a natural change. Then, turn toward it and make it part of your practice.

Now, let's look at a few more ways to practice while you move. Mindful movement can be extremely adaptable, available to meet your needs.

CHAPTER 11

VARIATIONS ON A THEME

Mantras: Repeating Words and Phrases

The word mantra comes from the Sanskrit language of India, which is used in many Buddhist texts. "Man" translates as "mind." "Tra" translates as "vehicle." Thus, a mantra is a vehicle for the mind, another option to use as an object of meditation.

In mantra practice, you repeat a word or phrase either silently or out loud in a rhythmic fashion. Use simple, clear phrases that are easy to remember.

My favorites include: *here now, tall strong,* and *no skunks.* I mean, who knows? Maybe it will ward off skunks.

I also use a mantra I learned at a Shinzen retreat: *om mani padme hum.* It translates to "Hail the jewel in the lotus," and comes from an ancient Buddhist text. That's lovely, but I chant it because it reminds me of pleasant time spent with other meditators.

If you play golf, silently chant a mantra while you're waiting on the slow foursome ahead of you. When I run, I time the mantra with my steps or my breath. In tennis, silently exhale a word while you serve. Or shout it. What the heck!

Mantra practice builds concentration and cultivates healthy mind states. "Metta" or "loving-kindness" meditation is a form of mantra practice using repeated phrases. Similar mantras can be used to return the mind to other wholesome mind states such as equanimity, empathetic joy, and compassion.

When I played golf with my father the year before he died of cancer, I created my own mantra to cultivate a sense of equanimity and chanted it under my breath whenever I began to panic:

In this moment, our bills are paid.

In this moment, Dad is still alive and not in pain.

In this moment, I get to be with him.

When you do mantra practice, don't try to replace the natural thoughts that arise in the mind. No need to try forcing out bad thoughts. Instead, test-drive helpful ones. No willpower, only gentle repetition. More nudge than shove. If you feel resistance to a phrase, acknowledge that. Make the resistance part of the practice, too.

Mantras for Mental Health

Centuries of anecdotal evidence and numerous scientific studies have proven that mantra practice calms the body's nervous system.

In one study from 2015 published in the journal *Brain and Behavior*, researchers found that study participants who engaged in mantra practice had decreased brain activity, which [in turn] fostered increased focus and relaxation, qualities that create conditions for good mental health.[30]

The study showed that "repetitive speech" (a mantra) was powerful enough to reduce brain activity even if no complex training was given. They found the impact on brain structures strong enough to explain the calming effect of mantra meditative practice and show why it was so popular "across cultural and historical boundaries."

While the movement practice itself will reduce anxiety, when combined with mantra practice, which is scientifically proven (and has historically been used) to calm the mind, you have an incredible method of stemming anxiety, whether at its roots or mid-attack.

Puzzle Practice

Doing puzzles in your head during a workout will also grow your concentration and equanimity. Notice any drive to find the answer. Drop that, and it becomes a form of "don't know mind."

I belong to a gym with an indoor track that is twenty laps to a mile. One of my favorite meditations is to reduce fractions. It helps me keep track of how many laps I've covered. I also carry a handheld click counter, but the fraction game keeps me focused and calm.

If I need to run four miles, that's 80 laps. After the first lap, I think "1/80." That can't be reduced. The second lap, 2/80, reduces to 1/40. The third lap, 3/80, can't be reduced. The fourth lap, 4/80, reduces to 2/40, which then reduces to 1/20. I'm 1/20 of the way through. If my mind wanders, I gently bring it back and then look at the clicker in my hand. If it says seven (7 laps), that's 7/80, which doesn't reduce. But 8/80 becomes 1/10. It's a focus

---

30   Aviva Berkovich-Ohana, Meytal Wilf, Roni Kahana, Amos Arieli, and Rafael Malach www. ncbi.nlm.nih.gov/pmc/articles/PMC4511287.

and mind state exercise and a way to pass the time. My friends joke that I have an infinite capacity for boredom. I nod and think, "I'm not bored. I'm meditating."

Do Nothing

I'm sick of all this instruction. I can't decide what to do. My mind hurts!

Great!

Time to do nothing.

Huh?

Shinzen teaches a practice he calls "Do Nothing." Other traditions call it "choiceless awareness" or "just sitting." The only instruction is, "Let whatever happens, happen. As soon as you're aware of an intention to control your attention—drop that intention."[31] It's the ultimate solution to the confusion and decision fatigue meditation can create. With time, and Shinzen puts heavy emphasis on that word *time*, "Do Nothing" helps quiet the part of you trying to control things, including your attention. Quiet will calm both your body and your mind.

How is this different from what I did before I learned to meditate?

The difference is that you have now learned to meditate. You used to be a cucumber, but you're turning into a pickle. There's no going back. Even if you've only done a teensy bit of meditation, some part of you knows what to do. This exercise lets that part take over.

---

31   Shinzen Young. unifiedmindfulness.com/wiki/index.php/%22Do_Nothing%22_
    Meditation_~_Shinzen_Young_(transcript).

YOUR TURN: DO NOTHING

Choose your movement form and your interval. For this exercise
only, don't choose an object of meditation. Instead, simply begin
to move. As you move, let your experience be exactly what it is.
Scattered? Fine. Sleepy? Fine. Don't try to change how you react.
Let your awareness go where it wants. Let your mind wander.
Any time you feel the urge to control any part of your experience,
including your attention, let that go too.

Summary

Mantras! Puzzles! Or, nothing! Oh my!

In the next section, I'll talk about the origins of this practice. I teach
movement meditation, but it wasn't my idea.

CHAPTER 12

WHOSE IDEA WAS THIS?

Buddhists Don't Worship Buddha

In the early 2000s, long before I took up running, I began to teach writing practice to adults in central Ohio. The class, based on Natalie Goldberg's work, included meditation. A few people balked at that. When I asked participants to raise their hands if they had ever meditated, four or five people in a class of thirty shyly put their hands in the air, then quickly put them down. Now, more than twenty years later, nearly every hand is raised.

But having meditation experience does not mean they understand the type of meditation I offer.

During one class a woman said, "I don't want to worship Buddha." I thanked her for bringing up this important point. Until she raised the issue, I hadn't realized people had this misconception. I want to clarify that and assuage any concerns about what this practice might mean to anyone's beliefs or understanding about their religion or other strongly held convictions.

Meditators in the Buddhist lineage that I practice don't worship the Buddha.

The Buddha was not a deity. While some Buddhists believe in reincarnation and some honor the Buddha in ways that look like worship, they simply emulate his practices.

People don't actually become Buddhists. That's a misnomer. Rather, we *do* Buddhist meditation. We become practitioners. Yes, there are Buddhist philosophies, concepts, ideas. But those are not intended to turn anyone into anything. Rather, they are intended to provide insight into who you really are. For some people, that might be more religious. For others, it might be less. You do not have to abandon any belief system you have or believe anything at all.

Meditation is simply a technique for investigating your body and mind, one that trains you to keep your mind where your body is, in the present moment.

Do not trust me. Trust only your own experience. Try the techniques and see what happens.

Who Was the Buddha?

The Buddha was a man or possibly the composite of a man or maybe a story about a man who lived in the fifth century BCE in India. Whether folklore or fact, the story most widely told is that he was a prince born into a wealthy family. His father wanted to shelter him from the world. And so, the boy who would become the Buddha did not see aging, sickness, or death.

But one day, the curious Buddha convinced his driver to take him outside the compound. Outside the walls, he saw the reality of life.

"What is that?" he asked, seeing a man throwing up in a pail.

"That man is sick."

"What is 'sick?'"

The driver explained that people sometimes get ill. They continued on.

"What is wrong with her?" he asked about an elderly woman walking with a cane, her white hair wrapped in a scarf.

The driver explained. "That is an old woman. We all age. Our bodies do not stay as they are now. It will happen to everyone." They traveled on.

Eventually, they came upon a funeral pyre. "What is this?" the Buddha asked.

"A person has died, and that is a funeral." Again, the Buddha was confused. The driver explained that all life would eventually cease. "Each of us will die."

The Buddha asked, "Even my father?"

"Yes, even your father. Even me. Even you."

The Buddha grew still. "Please take me back," he said. Upon his return, he vowed to end the suffering he had witnessed and left his rich dwelling, never to return.

On his quest to end suffering, the not-yet-Buddha joined different communities. At one point, he became an aesthetic, but that wasn't the solution. He joined a different group that worked with deep concentration, but he couldn't stay in the concentrated state forever. When he popped out of the trance, suffering returned.

Along his path, the soon-to-be-Buddha saw someone playing a stringed instrument. If the string was too loose, it would not sound. If it was too tight, it would break. It had to be just right: the middle way.

Eventually, the man who would become the Buddha sat down under a Bodhi tree (the tree of awakening). He sat and sat as wave after wave of temptation, confusion, and anger swept over him. The folklore says that

Mara, the ruler of the desire realm, sent temptation after temptation, trying to keep the Buddha from enlightenment.

There are many stories about the Buddha's eventual enlightenment. Here is my favorite:

For days and days, the Buddha sat through all the temptations, challenges, and mind tricks. As the would-be-Buddha continued to sit under the tree, Mara appeared, issuing one final challenge.

He put his face right in the Buddha's, and with all the anger he could muster, shouted, "Who are you to be the enlightened one?" hoping to instill the Buddha with unspeakable doubt.

But the Buddha had grown in equanimity; he had become unflappable. He did not open his eyes. He simply put his fingers to the ground, touching it softly with his fingertips. With the Earth as his witness, he said,

"I am here."[32]

For someone like me who, despite repeated success, has a mind that wants her to feel like an impostor in every area of life and who doubts herself at every turn, this story has more power than anything else. I am here. I show up. I do the work. That gives me the right to experience relief—if not an end to all my suffering, at least the lessening of suffering that meditation can bring.

What Causes Suffering?

Buddhism also gets a bad reputation for being negative. After all, loosely translated, the First Noble Truth in Buddhism is, "There is suffering." Who wants that? Much of the wellness industry is founded on the premise of escape: Realign, buy a gadget, learn a thing.

---

32 Author's Note: Most books about the Buddha's enlightenment include some variation of this story. I share this version, paraphrased from my decades of reading, because it means the most to me. Find the one that speaks to you.

Sometimes that works.

But what if it doesn't? What happens when the distraction only leaves you wanting more and the thing you learned stops working? What do you do when everything you try causes you to suffer? What then?

That's where meditation comes in. It suggests looking directly at the problem itself.

The basic premise of Buddhism is summarized in the Four Noble Truths:[33]

1. There is suffering.

2. Suffering is caused by craving and aversion.

3. If we can liberate ourselves from these desires of craving and aversion, suffering will cease.

4. The Noble Eight-Fold Path[34] is a method to become free from craving and aversion.

So, is meditation self-help?

Sort of; although Buddhists don't believe in a fixed state of "self," so there is no "self" to be helped. I'll discuss that later. For now, simply know that meditation is one part of the eight-fold path that can help to end suffering.

Let's define a few terms.

Craving

In short, craving means to want something. It's normal. You want to eat. You want to do well in your job. You might want a partner, or a dog, or both. And you might get all of those things.

---

33 "Buddhism for Beginners: Four Noble Truths" *Tricycle*. tricycle.org/beginners/buddhism/four-noble-truths.

34 "Buddhism for Beginners: Eight-Fold Path" *Tricycle*. tricycle.org/beginners/buddhism/eightfold-path.

But what happens when you get the thing? Is it enough? Or do you want more?

And what happens if you don't get the thing? Can you be okay with that? Perhaps outwardly. You move on. You get a different job. You learn to live alone. But what happens inside?

Craving happens on the inside. It's an internal pull on the psyche, a sense that you must have a thing. And it creates an imbalance.

Think about a food craving. We want chocolate, or coffee, or a beer, or that cheesy pizza slice we saw on that commercial. We feel it in our bodies. It pulls at us. The mouth waters. We might not even be hungry or thirsty, but there it is. We crave it.

Of course, the body is hardwired to keep us alive, and it needs food to do that. You might argue that food cravings only become a problem when we can't control those desires and we overeat or eat things that don't agree with us. But do you really enjoy something that has such a strong pull, even when it's not harmful?

That craving modality works all day long. "I want this. I want that. I want, want, want." Once you begin to pay attention to the craving feeling, you'll notice it everywhere. I want to sit in that chair. I want to drive a car like she has. I want to be with someone who looks like that. It's very unconscious. Meditation brings it to the surface. You experience it fully and allow it to eventually settle into its right place.

Aversion

Aversion is the opposite of craving. It is *not* wanting something. You don't want to be hungry. You don't want to live alone. You don't want the snake your partner wants as a pet.

Let's go back to food to see how this works. Think of the most repulsive thing, one you would never eat, something that makes your stomach turn. Ugh! That feeling? That's aversion. It's a very powerful, unpleasant, and strong sensation.

Similar to craving, aversion drives our lives. Aversions push us away from things. "I don't want that, or that, or that." I don't want to sit in that chair. I don't like to be cold. I don't want to be with someone who believes X, Y, or Z. I don't want a pet snake! Awakening to that in your daily experience, you'll realize how much energy you spend avoiding things you don't like. Subtle or strong, aversion is with you, prompting many of your actions.

Both craving and aversion are with us all day, with craving pulling and aversion pushing. That's the Second Noble Truth. "Desire," i.e., craving and aversion, causes suffering.

See, I warned you this can sound depressing. But I promise it's not all doom and gloom. Here's why.

The Third Noble Truth explains the way out. You can end suffering by eliminating (or at least reducing) these cravings and aversions.

The Fourth Noble Truth offers the solution—the Eight-Fold Path[35]—to deal with craving and aversion. Meditation is one of the eight parts of that path. Through meditation, we see craving and aversion as they are. We learn to be with them completely. We eliminate suffering, at least in part, by meditating.

Side Paths

At the risk of oversimplification, think of this form of meditation as a deep inner dive. Our goal is to go directly down into the depths, not being distracted by or taking any side paths. The further we go into the murky

---

35   "Buddhism for Beginners: Eight-Fold Path" *Tricycle*. tricycle.org/beginners/buddhism/
     eightfold-path.

water, the better. As the late Vietnamese Zen Master Thich Nhat Hanh said, "No mud, no lotus."[36]

Imagine a straight path down (or up, if you prefer). If you follow this path, you find calm, clarity, concentration, insight, compassion, and freedom from suffering along the way.

But, as with most things, distractions will arise.

One such distraction is bliss.

I know. Bliss is supposed to be good. But wanting bliss too much can create problems. The heightened states of awareness that come with meditation can cause spontaneous pleasure. After experiencing the positive sensations that arise around bliss, a meditator may become obsessed with recreating it. Craving the bliss leads to frustration at not being able to access it on demand. This causes suffering. Insight fails, and some may become disillusioned and begin to think meditation doesn't help.

When pursued, that bliss, a natural consequence of meditation, becomes a side path many people travel at great length. This path may circle back to the main road, the middle way. When that center is recognized, the seeking can be abandoned and a firm course on the path toward the end of suffering may resume.

Another side path may be visions or even hallucinations.

At one retreat with Shinzen Young, shortly after my father died, I eagerly shared a recent meditation experience. Sitting cross-legged on our sofa, deep in meditation, I had heard my father encourage me. I often fight self-doubt. It haunts me. It's my constant companion. I opened my eye slightly and could almost make out a tall shape I immediately recognized as my father. I closed my eyes, not wanting the vision to disappear.

---

36   Thich Nhat Hanh. *No Mud, No Lotus: The Art of Transforming Suffering.* (Berkeley: Parallax Press, 2014).

And I began to talk to my father, sharing my confusion with my career. After speaking quietly for a moment, I called out.

"Dad? Should I keep writing?"

As clearly as if he were right there, I heard him say, "Go for it."

I opened my eyes. The vision was gone, but our little white dog Astro was looking at the space where the vision had been.

When I told Shinzen about this experience, he reminded me of the tricks the mind plays during deep states of concentration.

"I'm not saying you didn't see your father. It's more important to ask, 'Can you infuse this experience with awareness and equanimity?' Also, 'Can you feel the craving for more arise in you?' And finally, 'Are you aware of the suffering this craving causes?'"

I did not want to hear that! My experience was and is very real to me. I still feel as if my dead father told me not to give up on writing.

But Shinzen wasn't talking about the content of my vision. He was talking about my internal reaction to it.

Through practice, Shinzen wanted me to develop the ability to see my dead father stand before me, hear him speak the very words I most desired, and experience that fully without needing more. Craving and excitement kept me from being present. And my desire for my father's approval turned every meditation session for a long time after into a deep well of need.

A different teacher in a different tradition might have offered tools to help me stay in touch with my father. In some traditions, people speak with the dead, see visions, and conjure images.

But those paths to the left or right, not along the middle way, might lead to more suffering. Shinzen's tradition, Vipassana, teaches that middle way. While it broke my heart that day, his questions were spot on.

Finger Pointing to the Moon

Having written all this, I laugh at myself because I feel grasping in my own words. I make it sound as if the path is clear and straight. It sounds like the highway to heaven.

No. Sometimes, it is the opposite.

It's nearly impossible to make sense of this with your mind. It must be experienced. As the Buddha is claimed to have said, "The teachings are but a finger pointing to the moon."[37]

Still, continue to point I shall.

Summary

This wasn't my idea. The principles behind mindful movement meditation originated centuries ago in India, developed by the Buddha. You don't need to become a Buddhist to meditate. And you don't need to believe me. You learn who you are by tuning into your own experience in a way you haven't before. You only need to believe your own experience.

In the next section, we circle back to the very first step in *How to Meditate While You Move*, choosing a movement practice. People have questions, and I do my best to answer.

---

37 "What the 'Finger Pointing to the Moon' analogy really means—from Zen Buddhism, the Buddha in the Shurangama Sutra.'" essenceofbuddhism.wordpress.com/2016/04/19/what-the-finger-pointing-to-the-moon-analogy-really-means-from-zen-buddhism-the-buddha-in-the-shurangama-sutra.

CHAPTER 13

MORE ABOUT FORMS OF MOVEMENT

Which Form?

Is one movement form better for meditation?

Are there basic requirements for a form to be transformed into meditation?

How should I choose a movement form?

Where and how do I start?

Sorry (not sorry) to sound like a broken record, but it depends. On what does it depend? You!

I'm not a fan of, "No pain, no gain." But some discomfort can't be avoided. We take care to use the right amount of effort without causing unnecessary pain.

I enjoy running, think of myself as a runner, and identify with the running crowd. But as I age, I'm not as fast as I used to be. Races I used to enjoy become tedious and boring. I respect that, own it, and adapt. If running ever becomes impossible, I will find another movement form.

Movement, not the type, matters. It's only important that you move.

Please consider this. We think we love an activity or environment. In fact, the thing we enjoy is concentration. Our brains crave focus. They want the calm that comes from being deeply immersed in a task even if parts of it are unpleasant.

While your finances, physical stamina, previous injury level, and/or your personality may cause you to prefer one activity over another, the real answer is it doesn't matter.

Bottom line? The *best* activity for you, the prime movement form, the perfect one for transformative meditative practice, is *the one you will do*.

Posture

Much of the literature about meditation discusses sitting practice and emphasizes the importance of sitting posture. Sitting is one of the three postures the Buddha discussed. He also talked about lying down and standing. I doubt the Buddha forgot about movement. Thich Nhat Hanh sure didn't. He made walking meditation popular. Many other meditation teachers talk about it, too:

> "Walking is the great adventure, the first meditation, a practice of heartiness and soul primary to humankind. Walking is the exact balance between spirit and humility."
>
> —Gary Snyder[38]

The "posture" principles emphasized in sitting also apply to movement practice. In running, I work with ChiRunning form: light feet, lengthening from my spine, pelvis slightly tilted forward, high foot turnover (cadence),

---

38   Gary Snyder, *The Practice of the Wild* (Berkeley: Counterpoint Press, 2010), 19.

and falling forward from my center of energy, the center of gravity, a point just below the naval. I either choose one aspect of form to note or shift my awareness between several aspects.

What makes posture important?

In sitting meditation, good posture aids clarity and calmness. You are upright and awake but relaxed like that instrument string, not too tight and not too loose. This removes distractions, lessens hindrances, and facilitates meditation.

The suggested posture increases the likelihood that you will have experiences similar to those millions of people who have meditated before you, including the Buddha, whether experiences of simple insight or full-on enlightenment. The posture creates an environment that enhances those possibilities.

Posture also matters in movement meditation. It helps you stay alert, fully engaged, relaxed, and grounded. Every fitness discipline has a posture, usually called technique. This physical manifestation helps you be better at the sport. If you want to improve a movement activity, learn and practice the technique.

Technique may also help you find your object of meditation. In golf, it might be the swing. In tennis, also swing, but movement and footwork too. In dance, footwork, arm movements, and facial gestures if we're talking tango. In basketball, football, soccer, or other team sports, the dynamics grow even more, but within that overall movement, there are postures: postures within the main posture, movements within movement.

A basketball player uses similar movements when at the foul line and in the jump shot: the upward thrust of the arms, hand-eye coordination, and so on. But between those two movements exist degrees of difference. On the court, a player might attend to the shifting of weight from one foot to another, the moment of pushing off, and the follow-through, with the free throw different from the three-pointer.

Important aspects are specific to each movement form. Even in an aerobics class you take for fun and fitness, with no intent to compete, mastering the form makes it easier. That pleasure is another serious fruit of practice.

You may experience discomfort learning the posture (i.e., the movement). If so, make discomfort part of your practice. Think of it as *right effort*, and it might not feel as annoying or disheartening. Weave it into the meditation.

You might feel self-conscious learning a new movement form or trying to improve one you already do. In meditation, Shinzen calls this part of the "awkward intermediate stages."[39] We've all experienced them.

When I attempt a new ChiRunning form focus, I feel clumsy. "Do I even know how to run?" This from a woman who has run thousands of miles. I know how, just not this way. When you get used to moving in a particular way, you go on autopilot. Bringing attention to each movement can feel awkward. If so, make the thoughts and body sensations of awkwardness your object of meditation.

But I Don't Move

But don't you?

You walk to the bathroom to brush your teeth. You walk to the pantry to feed the dog and into the kitchen to make coffee. You walk to the back door to let the dog out. And on and on, you walk all day long. Ordinary, garden variety walking counts as movement. Want it to count more? Walk more.

You bend...over to tie your shoes.

You stretch...your arm over your head when you take an object off a high shelf.

---

39   Shinzen Young, What to Expect and Do After a Mindfulness Retreat ~ Shinzen Young
     (transcript). unifiedmindfulness.com/wiki/index.php/What_to_Expect_and_Do_After_a_
     Mindfulness_Retreat_~_Shinzen_Young_(transcript).

You twist...your arm when you reach for a doorknob and your wrist when you turn it.

See! You're already moving.

That's not what I meant!

Oh, I know.

We have ideas about what exercise *should* be and what we *should* be doing and what it *should* look like (*and what we should look like*). I invite you to drop those. Since you might not be able to easily dump your expectations of what exercise should be, let's work toward something different. Open your mind to everything movement might entail.

Here's my definition of exercise: doing ordinary movement in a structured way, on purpose.

A few tips:

1. *Look for a form that suits your personality*. Do you need competition or achievement? Do you prefer to be in a group or alone? Do you like intense activity or something slow and methodical? Do you need variety or does repetitive motion soothe you? There is a movement form for every personality.

2. *Tie it to something you already do*. Brush your teeth every day? Stretch while you brush. Do you take the kids to school weekdays? Instead of driving home, drive to the park and run a few loops on the trail. Working through your lunch breaks? Walk around the building (inside or outside) before you eat.

3. *Take a dare*. In *The Four-Hour Body*, Tim Ferriss writes about the success factor of making a bet. Search "exercise bet" online for an array of virtual options. Go old school and dare a friend. Or watch for challenges I issue in my email newsletter. Money on the line might help, but a simple, "I dare you..." might work.

And please. Don't wait to find a movement form until you experience something as serious as a depressive episode so severe it makes you contemplate ending things. The most important thing is to choose a form you enjoy and will do.

What About Yoga?

What about types of movement typically thought of (or touted) as meditative? Should I choose yoga, qigong, or tai chi? Do certain movement forms particularly lend themselves to mindfulness and meditative states?

You do not need to choose a movement form traditionally thought of as meditative unless it appeals to you. Anything we do or don't do can serve as a container in which to meditate. Use everything.

The real question is, are you meditating when you do the movement? The movement itself is not meditation. What matters is what you do with your mind. Where is your attention while you move?

Yoga, tai chi, certain dance forms, and healing practices such as Feldenkrais, Alexander Technique, and others might seem easier to turn into meditative movements, but they are not always better options.

Yoga specifically comes from a similar root as Buddhist meditation. Early texts share common language, and some meditation teachers even refer to their students as "yogis."

As a result, there is overlap between yoga practice and meditation. Some yoga teachers offer the type of meditation practice I suggest. Other yoga teachers focus more on postures and do not instruct students to focus attention inside the body. They may not teach equanimity or the development of mind states.

Similarly, martial arts such as tai chi and qigong have common roots with Buddhist meditation. Again, depending on the instructor, a student of these arts might learn meditation skills. Or the sessions might be more about physical exercise than the inner workings of the mind.

Movement alone is not meditation. While it is possible to slip into a meditative state without instruction, especially if you naturally excel at concentration and the movement form requires focus for your safety or encourages it for your enjoyment, I want you to learn to meditate on purpose.

Of course, the mind looks for *perfect* because the mind likes *easy*. It may also look for a reason to stop you from meditating at all. Tricky, tricky mind. Be awake to any thought telling you that you can't meditate because of X, Y, or Z.

And no. Asking this question doesn't mean you don't want to meditate. You are not necessarily making excuses (though you could be!) It might mean you haven't yet fully grasped the definition of meditation I use in this book. And, it might mean you haven't yet experienced the benefits.

This is another reason meditation is the most adaptable well-being tool in the world. It fits any activity or non-activity. We can transform anything into a meditative practice.

Pick One

The movement form you choose is not as important as the act of choosing one. And choosing a form is even less important than actually doing it. Once you've found one you like, I recommend staying with it until you get the hang of making the movement a meditation.

Why?

Familiarity reduces awkwardness. Yes, we can meditate on awkwardness, but when you become familiar with a form, it's easier to go deeper into the practice.

Your personality may dictate this. While I like to do the same thing over and over, not everyone does. They might need to change it up, switch movement forms, or make changes within the practice. I choose different routes or run at different speeds.

Choosing one form allows you to dive in. You won't need to think about how to do the form itself while you're doing your movement meditation. Not having to think about the form allows you to concentrate and build equanimity.

For example, if you already play badminton and know the rules, using badminton as a movement meditation form allows you to deepen your concentration within the form, and also lets you awaken to subtle changes you might not see if you were learning the rules.

Specific Sports

How do other longtime meditators do movement practice?

Members of the Shinzen Young Mindfulness Community Facebook group[40] answer this question here.

Daron Larson, a meditation coach, offered this list for *weight lifting* practice:

---

40   Shinzen Young Mindfulness Community Facebook Group: www.facebook.com/groups/shinzenyoungmindfulnesscommunity.

"1) Super slow repetitions. Holding at top and bottom of each one. Trying to have equanimity with discomfort that appears in the middle of a rep. 2) When doing regular paced weight lifting, noticing as the muscle gets more fatigued as you do repetitions. 3) Noticing the subtle, pleasant sensations related to fatigue and increased blood flow at the end of a workout."

—Daron Larson[41]

Jeff Sinclair, who plays *ice hockey* as a goalie, uses meditation to stay focused and on an even emotional keel during a fast-paced game:

"I focus on my breath, on the puck, and the other players; if I have thoughts, I can label them See or Hear and not get wrapped up in them and taken out of the moment. Also, I can use the Auto move techniques because most of my saves are pretty automatic. I just watch the puck as it comes in, and my body automatically makes the moves I need to make a save."

Jeff Sinclair[42]

Jeff uses labels from Unified Mindfulness,[43] a meditation program created by Shinzen Young.

41　Daron Larson, Comment on Shinzen Young Mindfulness Community Facebook Group Post.

42　Jeff Sinclair, Comment on Shinzen Young Mindfulness Community Facebook Group Post.

43　Unified Mindfulness. unifiedmindfulness.com.

Alan Francis says this about practicing while he plays *snooker*, a game similar to pool:

> "I am at my best in a meditative state. Whilst awaiting my turn, I either observe my breath or keep my attention on the table. When my turn comes, parts of my body—feet, arms, hands—grab my attention. Whilst playing the cue, the table and balls are all part of my attention. I use the sensations of touch and vision. There is not a bad shot or good shot. I try to treat them all the same. My opponent is really me. If I don't feel right today and my game is off, I observe that feeling with equanimity."
>
> —Alan Francis[44]

Patrick Dement shares the objects of meditation he attends to while *dancing*:

> "Shifting weight, stepping, lifting a leg, moving arms, literally everything. Tuning in to feel sensations, noticing flow, hearing the music."
>
> —Patrick Dement[45]

---

44 Alan Francis, Comment on Shinzen Young Mindfulness Community Facebook Group Post.

45 Patrick Dement, Comment on Shinzen Young Mindfulness Community Facebook Group Post.

Suzie Loveday described mindful *sailing*:

> "When sailing, especially on night watch, mindfulness was almost
> entirely focused on internal perceptions. The wind was felt on
> the front, back, left, and right of the body. [I noticed] what the
> waves were doing—felt in feet, legs, and hips. Strength of current
> felt through hand, strength needed to keep the wheel steady. If
> we were close to land, through smell or bird sounds: a welding of
> body, boat, and nature to steer our course."
>
> —Suzie Loveday[46]

Brad Constable practices while doing *physical therapy* exercises for lumbar stenosis. He focuses on body sensations around releasing muscles from nerve root compression while he does *pigeon-pose* or other *yoga*-type stretches.[47]

Jim Smith does several types of movement meditation, including a *relaxation exercise* where he moves each part of the body ten times to relieve muscle tension. He also does *walking* or *cycling* meditation when he goes to the grocery. Jim observes the physical feelings of moving and builds concentration by counting repetitions.

As far as building equanimity, Jim says:

> "[I include it] the same way I would in any situation where
> unpleasant thoughts, emotions or feelings might arise. I try not to
> push away or get carried away into mind wandering or accepting
> the unpleasantness as any kind of 'truth.' "
>
> —Jim Smith[48]

---

46 Suzie Loveday, Comment on Shinzen Young Mindfulness Community Facebook Group Post.

47 Brad Constable, Comment on Shinzen Young Mindfulness Community Facebook Group Post.

48 Jim Smith, Comment on Shinzen Young Mindfulness Community Facebook Group Post.

He sometimes grows impatient; when he does, he notes that. He also labels for concentration:

> "When my mind is turbulent, I may label movements: 'stepping,' 'reaching,' 'turning,' etc. I don't try to label everything because I try to keep a relaxed rhythm. When my mind is calmer, I will just be aware of moving and balance.
>
> If something unpleasant arises and I feel a resistance to observing it, I look at the resistance. That's often productive because it takes you down to a lower layer of emotion. When I get to the bottom layer, I often find an inconvenient truth about myself, and consciously recognizing and accepting those inconvenient truths is a way of surrendering that frees you from a lot of cognitive dissonance (suffering)."
>
> —Jim Smith[49]

And Jim attends to his personal safety outdoors, as I hope we all will:

> "Outside with traffic and people around, there can be a lot of distractions. I have to pay attention to traffic mindfully. I watch the road and listen for traffic as well as breathing in a relaxing way, trying to stay relaxed, and noticing emotions that may arise. When something causes stress, I try not to push it away, I let it express itself, but I also try to stay mindful and not get distracted by mental wandering or thinking the emotion is anything real other than a feeling in my mind/body. Emotions are not truths or logical."
>
> —Jim Smith[50]

Patricia Houser uses noting as motivation on the *treadmill*:

---

49   Jim Smith, Comment.

50   Jim Smith, Comment.

"A lot of times I don't feel like exercising. So when I'm on the treadmill, I'll label the emotion I'm feeling and just repeat it. I'll get into a rhythm of sorts, saying, 'crappy, crappy, crappy.' Sometimes I'll just make up a word. It works! I'm heavily influenced by Shinzen Young's CD *Pain Relief*[51] from years ago."

—Patricia Houser[52]

Pez Owen teaches *mindful hiking* to small groups. He guides them to note vision, body sensations, and sound. He also meditates during *laser tag*![53]

Victor Cotea practices *Brazilian Jiu Jitsu*, but he works to integrate meditation into all life activities, including sports and physical exercise. In Jiu Jitsu, he uses the visual field and his body as the object of meditation. If a certain window opens, he does Metta practice:

"I keep my awareness as broad as possible, trying to cover the whole space (of mostly seeing and feeling) simultaneously. Brazilian Jiu Jitsu is physically intense, and there is a lot of contraction happening both in the body and in the mind (at least at my beginner-intermediate level). Any time I make conscious contact with body or with seeing-space, I aim to zoom out to cover the whole field."

—Victor Cotea[54]

He intentionally creates equanimity by defocusing his gaze during sparring and by intentionally relaxing his body when it's appropriate.

---

51   Shinzen Young, *Natural Pain Relief*, audio CD, (Boulder: Sounds True, 2011).

52   Patricia Houser, Comment on Shinzen Young Mindfulness Community Facebook Group Post.

53   Pez Owen, Comment on Shinzen Young Mindfulness Community Facebook Group Post.

54   Victor Cotea, Comment on Shinzen Young Mindfulness Community Facebook Group Post.

"Jiu Jitsu techniques are subtle and complex. The whole experience can be sensorially busy. It takes a strong determination and good momentum of mindfulness skills to touch base into mindful awareness during training."

—Victor Cotea[55]

When I asked Victor if he meditated for the entire workout, he laughed:

"I wish! I mostly touch base with moments of mindful awareness through noting whenever I can. It's a discontinuous process. A window of opportunity opens during instruction or a break when we wait or recover. I focus on restful mind and body states. I zoom out, dissolve the sense of boundary of my body between outside and inside (the best I can), and from that point of feeling spaciousness in the body, quite often a sense of gratitude and appreciation arises (being with friends, training, getting better together). I use that feeling of (let's say) 'Metta' as an object of meditation, letting it spread in all directions around me."

—Victor Cotea[56]

Tennis player and coach Kika Cicmanec practices this way:

"When I play, I focus my attention on the sound of hitting the ball. I stay with that for a while, then shift my attention to the feeling of hitting the ball, and then I switch to really watching the ball (how it spins, almost wanting to see it in slow motion). So, I sprinkle micro-hits throughout my session."

—Kika Cicmanec[57]

---

55   Victor Cotea, Comment.

56   Victor Cotea, Comment.

57   Kika Cicmanec, Facebook Direct Message.

She takes a slightly different approach when *lifting weights*:

"When I struggle with fatigue through a set, I redirect my attention away from feeling exhausted and thinking how hard it is and focus solely on the muscle I am using for the exercise. This makes me forget that I was thinking I was exhausted and gives me an extra push to finish the set. I'm always amazed how changing the direction of attention to what the muscle does changes your whole experience and makes the exercise easier."

—Kika Cicmanec[58]

Andrew McMillan shared how they select an object of meditation during different phases of *aerobic exercise*:

"Awareness of breath when doing aerobic exercise. Expanded field of vision and auto move for rock climbing (to counteract the way focus will try and bring location to a specific visual point). Expanded vision and feel flow when going downhill on a mountain bike or skiing."

—Andrew McMillan[59]

CrossFit **enthusiast Juan Samuel Sangüesa Massiel explained his process:**

"I apply 'UM' techniques while doing CrossFit. For example, hear in (with background equanimity with feel out) when I have to count reps and endure a hard workout."

—Juan Samuel Sangüesa Massiel[60]

---

58 Kika Cicmanec, Direct Message.

59 Andrew McMillan, Comment on Shinzen Young Mindfulness Community Facebook Group Post.

60 Juan Samuel Sangüesa Massiel, Comment on Shinzen Young Mindfulness Community Facebook Group Post.

At one Shinzen retreat, meditation teacher W. T. S. Tarver created an exercise rubric for the meditators to follow if they chose. Those attending meditated while doing *calisthenics*, including jumping jacks, sit-ups, push-ups, and burpees. Both the physical exercises and the meditation techniques increased in complexity each day of the retreat. Participants reported that even during the most strenuous exercises, they could find stillness in their minds and bodies.[61]

Summary

There are unlimited options for movement forms to use as meditation. Choosing a movement form need not be complex. Make it easy. Find one you love—one you'll do—and make that your practice.

Next, let's look at how to customize your movement meditation and make it truly yours. Dr. George A. Sheehan, a famous runner who was also a physician, said, "Each of us is an experiment-of-one."[62] While this practice has existed for thousands of years, never before was there a *you* doing it. Let's look at how to make it your own.

---

61   W.T.S. Tarver, telephone conversation.
62   Dr. George Sheehan, "Did I Win?" (1993). www.georgesheehan.com/essays/did-i-win.

CHAPTER 14

MAKE IT YOURS

Loving It

When Dr. Dan Skinner, editor-in-chief of *World Medical & Health Policy*, interviewed me on his *Prognosis Ohio* podcast for WCBE, a local NPR station, he said he hated running. He said it more than once. Maybe he wanted me to talk him into running, but I did not try. I said, "You might not be a runner."

Never force yourself to do a type of movement that doesn't interest or suit you. Choosing a practice is highly individual. It helps if you break a sweat, but it's more important to enjoy it.

Go to YouTube and search for "Prancercise." It's beyond my ability to describe it. Go look—you'll thank me. I love the comment: "Here is someone who doesn't try to be anyone but herself."[63] Let that be your goal. If you decide to Prancercise around your house (or bravely outdoors where someone might see), please let me know. Video not required, but I'd love one.

---

63   Comment by "bmo" on Prancercise Video, 2017. www.youtube.com/watch?v=o-50GjySwew&t=8s.

Explore different movement forms. If you bore easily, you probably won't
stick with repetitive activity. If you enjoy competition, you might need a
sport like handball, tennis, or racquetball in which you quickly know who
wins, although observing thoughts and body sensations around boredom or
losing is also great practice.

Embrace what you know about yourself. Whether you like to compete with
yourself or others, need time alone, or instead crave community, find it. If
you love a mental challenge alongside the physical challenge, you need a
sport that requires strategy as well as physical activity. Love geometry? Golf
might be your game. Time for trial and error.

Solo time running the roads with the companionship of the pupperina
makes running my perfect sport. Still, I need connection and support, so I
joined a group. But even on our Saturday group runs, you'll find me lagging.
I might start with the group, but usually wind up falling back and either
joining one other person or running solo. The group provides water for all,
as well as the safety in numbers a woman unfortunately needs. I enjoy those
benefits while doing my own thing.

Get creative. Find your way.

The meditation leadership program I attended, Sage Institute for Creativity
and Consciousness, emphasized the creativity part of practice. I loved that.
When we allow ourselves to be inventive, it adds a bit of delight that keeps
us coming back.

At first though, you might have to slow the movements of your chosen
sport. You might not be able to meditate in motion in a deeply concentrated,
mindful way while moving quickly. You might need to start with a slower
activity such as walking or do your favored activity in slow motion in order
to maintain calm, concentration, and clarity.

Another option is to only meditate during intervals. I mentioned this above
when I talked about choosing a time period. In the beginning, that interval

might need to be short in order for you to maintain your concentration and equanimity and grow your meditation skills.

"Be gentle with yourself. Be kind to yourself. You may not be perfect, but you are all you've got to work with. The process of becoming who you will be begins first with the total acceptance of who you are."

—Bhante Gunaratana, *Mindfulness in Plain English*[64]

The Record Book

Another way to make movement meditation yours is by keeping a record. This could be simple digital statistics recorded by a movement tracking tool or something else that lets you keep private notes.

While my Garmin watch records physical stats like pace, distance, and heart rate, I record what's going on inside me. After most workouts, I do writing practice. In addition to recording the stats, I track emotional changes and record aches, pains, and bliss. I see what's working and where I could improve. If I tried something new, I record that and say whether I would try it again.

I also track mood, energy level, chosen technique, reactions, mind state, and body state. If I was outdoors, I note the weather, the temperature, and my reaction to it.

My object of meditation and any challenges go in as well. Did I struggle with focus? How's my equanimity? Did any hindrances come up? I include sensory details. Were the challenges physical, emotional, or mental, and what was my response? If I hated something, I record the thoughts and body

---

64 Bhante Gunaratana, *Mindfulness in Plain English*, 47.

sensations that made up that emotion. I might look at the 5 Conditions and see if I've created a story I need to drop.

I also love to describe each dog, what breed, who was with them, and how Scarlet responded (e.g., bouncing, panting, and jumping).

It's often simple:

> Five miles in the fog with the pupperina. Chose open vision. Saw
> a skunk. Body tensed. Remembered to see the actual skunk, not
> thoughts. Black fur, white stripe, wormy, wiggly movement. She
> was quicker than I expected. Adorable and terrifying. I felt aversion,
> fear, curiosity, and wonder. Relaxed into it. Unpleasant sensations
> passed. So did the skunk.

In this private space, I can look back and see how it's going. If I'm working with a teacher or a trainer, I might share these notes to get feedback.

When I click save on an entry, it gives me a tiny dopamine hit. When I used to write them by hand, the feeling of ink flowing across the paper generated joy. I noticed that, too.

Start Where You Are

Pressure. Pressure. Pressure. Look left. Look right. Everywhere you turn, messages shout that you are not enough exactly as you are. Improve yourself. Work on yourself. Fix yourself.

If you're prone to any mental health condition, these messages hit hard. Many of us already struggle with conditions some people think are either imagined or our fault. These messages can sound like: "If only you worked harder, changed the way you thought, ate better, or read a different book..." (Excluding the book you're holding, naturally.) Or "If only X, Y, or Z, then you would be fine," or the mirror-image alternative: "You're doomed, resigned to be miserable." I urge you to turn away from this.

If you get any one single thing out of this book, please get this:

You are enough exactly as you are.

Maybe you feel called to meditate, meditation simply interests you, you think meditation might help your mood (there's science behind that, after all), or you're bored with crocheting or whatever. For some reason, you picked up this book and want to try a movement meditation practice.

You can do this!

After all, meditation, while helpful, is not about improvement. It is nearly the opposite. Meditation is not turning away. It is turning toward. It is not tightening. It is opening.

And this starts with accepting yourself.

You might not be there yet. You might rage as you read this. Or these words might make you feel sad, numb, or blah. Please don't turn away from those emotions.

If you're not where you want to be, that only means you're not where you want to be. That's all. Look at that. Feel that. Be with that.

That's where you start. That's what's here. *Here* is where you start.

Power of Choice

When I was at my worst emotionally, I didn't feel I had many choices. I knew a few things I didn't want, but I didn't feel I had the power to choose. I was on autopilot, surviving.

I never want to forget that feeling.

I don't want to replicate it. It was the opposite of fun. But I never want to forget I have choices.

I did have choices at that time, but mental health symptoms kept me from believing that. I felt trapped. It took me nearly ending my life to climb out of that trap. Voluntarily going to the behavioral health hospital (as opposed to against my will) was the first step in my mental health recovery.

Choices empower. That's why I encourage you to make this practice your own. It is a step forward. You claim a thing, invest time and energy in it. Spending time and attention on it gives it power.

That's why it's so important to develop focus and concentration. If you can't focus, you can't choose.

Even if your circumstances limit your choices, you still have options. If you can't go outside because it is not safe, if you don't have access to equipment, if you have trouble concentrating because of a medication, or if you have children, elderly parents, or an ailing spouse, you still have options. If you have limiting circumstances, even within those, I hope you see the choices you still have. They may not be ideal, not what you might want, or what I wish for you. But even with those limits, there are choices.

Here are some examples:

Raising children: The object of meditation becomes the touch of your clothes as you lift the baby out of the crib.

While caregiving: The object of meditation can be the sound of medical equipment, perhaps the whir of a food pump or the steady beat of the heart monitor. I did this in 2020 when Ed had a heart attack and open-heart surgery and was on a feeding tube for many months.

In a confined space: The workout becomes jumping jacks, push-ups, chair dips, lunges, or yoga on a rag rug.

With medication issues: The object becomes noticing any irritation that arises when you attempt a practice and cannot do it.

Choices might be internal. Can't change the outside circumstances? Turn inward. Make it part of the practice.

Recycle the reaction!

Summary

```
YOUR TURN: LET'S DANCE

Let's dance. Five minutes. In your socks. Just do it.

Who cares if they're watching?

Self-conscious? Notice that.

Happy? Notice that.

Both? Notice both.
```

Find a movement you love. Infuse that movement experience with awareness and equanimity, and meditation will rarely be a struggle.

Whether it's game day or match day or race day or recital day, if you have a big day when you want to excel, your movement meditation practice can be part of that experience. It's not just for practice. It's also for practice on the big day. Let's look at that next.

CHAPTER 15

TAKING IT ON THE ROAD

Your Big Day

What about my big day?

Oh, yes! For those of you who compete in your sport, race day, game day, match day, recital day or the day of any competition is where you take your movement practice on the road.

Before a race, if I've trained well, my coach says, "Trust your training." Those hours of movement meditation practice before the big day will serve you. Trust them. You will show up as prepared as possible, physically and mentally. You have internalized the meditation process. That training will carry you. Trust that, too. And while we both know it's not just another day, take that attitude as much as you can. Show up the same way you did during training.

Remind yourself of what you have learned. As you get dressed, gather your gear, and drive or walk to the start, be mindful. Once you arrive, stay focused. Warm up. Do some dynamic stretches. Jog around a bit. Wiggle your arms and legs. Charlie Watts, the late, legendary drummer for the

Rolling Stones, did a warmup routine in which he jiggled his legs and did arm circles in a style he had seen jazz dancers do before a show. I do "body looseners" I learned in ChiRunning, short movements to warm the muscles and remind my mind and body that it knows what to do. Warm up with attention. Keep your mind focused. Feel any excitement. Remain open and calm.

Spend a few minutes practicing focus. One golfer inks a dot on his glove. Before each shot, he stares at the dot, giving it all his attention. This concentration allows him to be completely present when he hits the ball. A basketball player sits on the bench, eyes down, giving all her attention to a speck on the floor. She's meditating, practicing concentration before going into play.

Try these preparations. Then, when the competition begins, you're all in. You won't have to think about being mindful. You already are.

Transitions

In the 1960s, people "dropped out." They dropped out of society and out of the general culture, using drugs to drop out of everyday consciousness. Meditation is your chance to "drop in," to be fully present with your life. There's no better time to do that than during your big event. When it's done on the fly during an activity, I call it "dropping in."

Find a reminder to help you "drop in," to bring your attention back to the present. Transitions work well. In a race, use mile markers. In a tennis match, a serve change or a point. In a game, any break in the action. Dancing? Let a change in the music signal your mind to drop in. Choose transitions that occur naturally. Use those as a gentle nudge, a reminder to bring yourself back.

This works in the rest of your life as well. Standing up after sitting? Notice. Walking through a doorway? Which foot went first? Let your movement practice spill over into the rest of your life.

A Poem

I wrote you a little poem. It begins:

> *Game Day*
> Success can boost your mood.
> Failure can bust your mood.
> Meditation teaches you to not be tossed away by either.

When I studied with Natalie Goldberg, she often recited three principals taught to her by Zen Master Katagiri Roshi:

> Continue under all circumstances.
> Don't be tossed away.
> Make positive effort for the good.[65]

They summarize the effort needed to follow any path, including movement meditation.

I wish I was no longer tossed away by either success or failure, but sometimes I still am. The impact of a big event depends on how I approach it. I still have big highs before a race, anxiety and excitement, and a letdown after, even if I do my best to stay mindful throughout. I can't imagine how a competition would knock my mood around if I didn't have movement meditation practice.

I remember my practice, which is, in effect, remembering myself. Here's the rest of the poem:

---

65   Natalie Goldberg, "Meet Your Life." Mountain Cloud Zen Center, March 18, 2021. www.mountaincloud.org/dharmatalk-meet-your-life.

During a race, I remember myself.

After the race, I remember myself.

Regardless of the outcome, I remember myself.

I let myself go. I let my *self* go. (More about that soon.)

Summary

YOUR TURN: BIG DAY

On your big day, incorporate some of these into your warmup:

Sharpen your focus by doing a concentration exercise. Count the breath. Stare at a dot on the floor. Chant a mantra. Practice being completely in your body. Scan your body. Build equanimity. Find a discomfort and open to it. If your nose or something itches, don't scratch it.

Events are lovely. They come and go. Practice is forever. After the event, return to practice.

Next, I'll address a somewhat confusing topic. Who's meditating? Who is experiencing and observing the thoughts and body sensations? Who are you?

CHAPTER 16

WHO'S MEDITATING?

Impermanence

A student once asked Shunryu Suzuki Roshi to summarize Buddhism in one sentence. Roshi's response?

"Everything changes."[66]

Impermanence.

Things well up. Do their little dance. Then pass.

Yet another way to define mindfulness meditation is the moment-to-moment awareness of impermanence. We see, smell, taste, hear, and feel things. We notice thoughts. And we notice that all those things (thoughts and body sensations) well up, do their little dance, and pass.

We are not exempt from impermanence. We too welled up (we were born). We do our little dance (live our lives). And we pass away. (Literally. One day each of us will die.)

---

66 Benjamin Riggs, "Everything the Buddha Ever Taught in 2 Words," *Elephant Journal*, May 12, 2014. www.elephantjournal.com/2014/05/everything-the-buddha-ever-taught-in-2-words.

Movement meditation helps us wake to this naturally occurring, infinite process. Attend to impermanence. Be with it. Let your experience happen, and even enjoy it. You are on a path to freedom.

Stillness in Motion

In addition to experiencing impermanence—how everything changes—we may also experience profound stillness. And we can experience this inner stillness while we move.

> "Silence is something that comes from your heart, not from outside. Silence doesn't mean not talking and not doing things; it means that you are not disturbed inside. If you're truly silent, then no matter what situation you find yourself in, you can enjoy the silence."
>
> —Thich Nhat Hanh, "The Heart of the Matter"[67]

W. T. S. Tarver, the meditation teacher who created that calisthenics routine for retreat attendees, also meditates while playing *disc golf*. He finds stillness as he prepares to throw the disc. In the moment before he releases it, everything stops. It's stillness in motion.

As I said before, in sitting practice, we are encouraged to still the body (by trying not to fidget) to encourage a calmer mind. Physical stillness creates conditions which allow thoughts and thinking to slow.

In movement, we create these conditions with relaxed concentration, a combination of focus and equanimity.

When you fully focus on your object of meditation, completely entranced by the body sensations or thoughts happening within your movement while

---

67 "The Heart of the Matter," *Tricycle*, Winter 2009, by Thich Nhat Hanh tricycle.org/magazine/thich-nhat-hanh-emotions.

remaining in relaxed equanimity, inner stillness can happen regardless of
what the body is doing. You experience the present moment as the only
reality. Distractions fall away. That sharpened awareness creates space.
When you attend to that space, it opens up even more space. Time may slow
or speed up. Mind fluctuations may also calm. Thoughts may even stop.

You've no doubt heard of the zone an athlete enters when completely
immersed in an activity. Because meditation is a natural mind state, this
might happen effortlessly. But intentional movement meditation allows
you to enter the zone on purpose. You find stillness within the movement
through this relaxed focus.

On a recent run, I worked on lengthening my head from the crown. That was
not my object of meditation. My object of meditation was any sensations
in my head and neck as I attempted this ChiRunning form, a subtle yet
important distinction. I attended to that felt sense in the physical body.

As I ran down the Olentangy Trail, noticing the bright orange and yellow
leaves and the occasional lime green ball of a fallen black walnut, I
repeatedly brought my attention back to the crown of my head, watching
for that lengthening sensation. I wasn't thinking about it. I was in my body,
experiencing the sensations: a slight tingle, a stretch, and a pleasant feeling
in the rest of my body when I felt that stretch lengthen.

When my mind wandered to the gorgeous trail scenery, I remembered my
chosen object of meditation. I reassured myself I wasn't missing anything.
I would run this trail again soon, and more leaves and walnuts would fall.
Back to the crown of my head. Back to the base of my head. Back to that
lengthening sensation.

Soon, I slipped into deep focus, inner stillness: nothing and everything all
at the same time. Yes, my arms swung from side to side as my feet hit the
ground. But within that movement, the crown of my head reaching skyward
felt still, calm, and silent. The more deeply I focused awareness on that

part of my body, the calmer the rest of me, including my mind, became. No reaching for anything. No craving. No aversion. Only the crown of my head.

I mentioned earlier that Shinzen often says, "Subtle is significant."[68] Mindful movement can bring seismic changes. More often, the change is incremental, much like the gradual progress concept of ChiRunning.

When we focus on a simple movement, attending to only one part of something complex, it encourages thoughts to slow. (It also reduces heart rate and blood pressure.) It's the opposite of our typical frenzied world.

The Experience of *No Self*

I heard a Buddhist teacher say, "There is no self." What the heck does that mean?

Some teachers won't explain it. They suggest you must experience it for yourself. And ultimately, you must. But I will tell you because I find it helpful.

The concept of *no self* is not as esoteric as it sounds. You may have already experienced it. If you've noticed the impermanence and stillness I mentioned, you're on the cusp of experiencing no self.

What meditation teachers mean by no self is not that there isn't a self. That would be ridiculous. After all, here I am writing this book, and here you are reading it.

What they mean is that what we call the "self" is a process, not a thing. The "experience of self" is the awareness of the arising, movement, and passing away of thoughts and body sensations. It is also the awareness of impermanence.

68   Shinzen Young, "Meditation: Escaping into Life—An Interview with Shinzen Young by Michael Toms." December 7, 2016. www.shinzen.org/wp-content/uploads/2016/12/art_escape.pdf.

After only a few years of meditation, I began to experience this process of a fluid self. By noticing how my thoughts and body sensations moved and changed, the concept of a solid, permanent "Nita" no longer matched my experience. That pain in my left knee? Not the hard knob I thought. Also, not "me," but just pain, which turned fluid and eventually passed.

That story I sometimes still tell myself about being too old, too fat, too slow, and "Who do you think you are?" is made of impermanent thoughts and body sensations that spiral and circle and feed off each other. If I hadn't realized those thoughts weren't real, that they weren't me, I would never have gotten beyond week four of Couch to 5k. Meditating while I run (or sit or dance or stretch) untangles the threads. Mindfulness shows each thought and body sensation for what it is—a passing phenomenon with a twinge of stillness now and then. The spiral slows and eventually stops. Talk about relief from suffering!

> "There is nothing more important to true growth than realizing
> that you are not the voice of the mind—you are the one who
> hears it."
> —Michael A. Singer, *The Untethered Soul: The Journey
> Beyond Yourself*[69]

To borrow a science analogy, you are more wave than particle. Seeing impermanence as you meditate helps you realize there is no fixed, concrete, solid "you" meditating. Sensations enter your sense gates, and your thoughts arise. The identity we call the "self" is formed by the awareness of that process, awareness of the impermanence of experience, the impermanence of thoughts and body sensations.

Seeing impermanence in action, and especially watching what you thought of as "you" fluctuate and change, is reassuring. The pain is not permanent.

---

69 Michael A. Singer, *The Untethered Soul: The Journey Beyond Yourself*, p. 10 (Oakland: New Harbinger, 2007).

The fatigue will subside. The swim meet will end. The race will be run. Eventually, you'll be able to get off the bike.

While you might grasp the ideas of impermanence and "no self" with your mind, you won't completely understand that *self* is a process until you watch your own experience arise, do its little dance, and pass away. Besides, there's nothing wrong with having a self. You absolutely have one. No *self*-hatred please! Although, if that arises, it's just one more thing to recycle into your practice.

Our movement meditation practice simply allows us to see this sense of self for what it really is, and that insight helps stop the emotional spiral. Our practice asks us to notice this process with the open-mindedness of equanimity. Observe without judging. Ask without needing to know the answer.

When you learn to stop identifying with your thoughts or body sensations and allow them to be, then you are in the moment. Rather than what you think you are or what you think you ought to be, you know who you actually are.

Self-Conscious

Self-consciousness is an "awkward intermediary phrase" of discovering that self is a process. Most of us go through the day on autopilot. You don't think: Lift your right arm. Grab the handle. Turn the knob. Pull the door toward you. Step through the opening. Turn back and close the door. Even typing that made me self-conscious. I had to slow down to capture each step. We usually do these steps automatically. This inner process runs in the background like a computer program we don't see when we have a different program maximized.

Look at that word: self-conscious—"self" and "conscious."

When the "self" arises, that unconscious process comes into awareness. Thoughts and body sensations, including emotions, bubble up.

Until the flow of thoughts and body sensations becomes apparent, this process controls us. We might be in denial about it and may have learned to ignore it. We're habituated. That negative voice we thought was normal and even helpful may actually be driving our mood into the ground. That's part of the *self* process. And that pit in the stomach when we think about getting injured and not being able to do our favorite movement, that too is an aspect of the *self* process.

That's why, when you try something new, you become "*self*-conscious"— conscious of your sense of *self*. That's the awkward intermediary phase.

At first, some people find this uncomfortable, while others enjoy seeing and feeling that sense of self arise and pass away in the natural fluctuations of experience.

Gone Meditation

YOUR TURN: GONE MEDITATION

Once I point you toward it, you might be surprised how easy it is to experience the impermanence of body sensations. We'll use the visual field again.

Start to move. As you do, choose an object that's ahead of you, but to your left or right.

If you're outdoors, you might choose a tree or a sign; if you're indoors, a piece of furniture or a picture.

Let the object take space in your visual field as you move toward it. Notice how it looks bigger as you move closer.

Eventually, you will pass it. While you know the object is still there behind you, that's a memory. The object is no longer in your vision. Only the memory remains. In your present moment consciousness, the object is "gone." Do this for whatever interval you like.

Gone meditation helps you experience impermanence. You can do gone meditation with other body sensations and thoughts as well. One of the most powerful "gone" meditations I've done was having an itchy nose and not scratching it. I got curious enough about it to let it itch. Eventually, without any action on my part, it stopped itching! The itch was *gone*!

After you build your concentration and equanimity, you can do gone meditation on the sense of self. You will notice that the self is simply a moving, changing constellation of thoughts and body sensations. It is the sinking feeling in your stomach in law school when the professor calls on you and you're not prepared to recite the facts of the case. It's the warm glow in your heart when your partner looks at you that certain way. And it's the cessation of both those things, usually with the passage of time.

Summary

I hope I didn't lose you in the no-self weeds. As you continue to practice, you will see impermanence and stillness. Your sense of a fixed, solid self may change. Regardless, continue to infuse your experience with awareness and equanimity. And continue to love your *self*, whether it's a wave, a particle, or (as it always is) grist for the mill!

Let's move on to the benefits of having expert help—meditation teachers and therapists—as well as the danger in becoming too much of an expert. I'll lay out some guidelines.

CHAPTER 17

WHY THERAPISTS HAVE THERAPISTS AND TEACHERS HAVE TEACHERS

You Might Need a Teacher

While this book teaches the basics of mindful movement meditation, nothing can replace a live human being to guide you in real time (whether in person or online). You might want to locate someone you trust, who is trained and can answer your questions. Even the most independent, self-sufficient, introverted athlete occasionally asks for help. The teacher or mentor you choose would also benefit from having their own teacher. It might not look like the traditional student-teacher role, but a good teacher has mentors on whom they rely.

No Self, No Problem

Despite my therapist's initial concern, my awareness of *no self*—seeing the impermanence of a fixed self—has not harmed my mental health. Rather, it allows me to see how the parts of me, especially those that aren't helpful, arise and pass away. I watch urges (healthy and unhealthy) well up and then pass, and I see that reactions pass when given enough time. It's life-affirming and fulfilling. Instead of feeling dead, I feel fully alive.

But remember Dr. Sheehan's motto: "We are each an experiment-of-one."[70] Some meditators experience the feeling of no self as alarming. Watching things pass can be threatening and sad. "Gone" meditation may bring up grief. While these deeper realms of the mind hold profound healing energies, the greater the mobilization, the more that these powerful energies of the psyche, including the shadow, move toward the surface.

As these obstructive and destructive forces become increasingly active, they can trigger a range of internal responses, including unconscious anxiety and defense systems long woven into the subtle fabric of our being. All of this is normal in the process of deepening practice. If not addressed, they could get worse over time: yet another reason to have contact with a teacher.

Most meditation instructions, including Shinzen's and mine, suggest making any difficulty part of the practice: Recycle the reaction. Generally, that works. But there's an underlying assumption:

To recycle it, you must have developed strong concentration and equanimity.

Choose a teacher trained in how to deal with trauma and unwanted side effects of meditation. Then do your part by staying in touch with the teacher. Let the teacher know if you have any experiences that worry or frighten you. This could be anything from heart palpitations to scary visual images. What one person finds concerning, another might enjoy. Use your judgment. If you're a beginning meditator, you might not know what to expect. Things that seem alarming could be normal. A skilled teacher can clarify.

If meditation causes any challenging symptoms, seek help from an experienced teacher, therapist, or other mental health professional. Again,

---

70   Dr. George Sheehan. "Did I Win?"

a symptom you find difficult might seem interesting to someone else. Don't be afraid to ask questions. Oddly enough, the treatment for adverse effects may include meditation. But that practice should be done under the direct supervision of a professional trained to deal with the condition. Please do not try that at home on your own.

Trauma

If you have a history of trauma, please work with a therapist who understands meditation. Also, let your meditation teacher know about your trauma history. Ask if they have experience dealing with trauma and the adverse effects that happen at times, although rarely. Check the Resources section of this book for more about this. You may also contact me at the email address in the back of this book. I'm not a therapist, but I am a trained meditation leader. I can share my own experience and direct you where to look for help. If you're in therapy, please talk to your therapist about mindfulness meditation.

Trauma-informed mindfulness meditation was developed after some people experienced depersonalization, a phenomenon where an individual's thoughts and sensations seem unreal to them. In trauma-informed meditation, the teacher instructs the meditator to turn toward pleasant experiences rather than unpleasant ones and to only dip into unpleasant experiences in small doses, in much the same way I dealt with my panic attack symptoms. I didn't know this was a thing when I did it, but it was very effective for me and has proven effective for others.

Please see a doctor sooner rather than later if you experience disturbing or emotionally disruptive symptoms or if your symptoms continue for a long period of time, and especially if they interfere with daily activities, relationships, or work. Your meditation teacher and your therapist can help, but other help is available. Check the Resources section for The Meditation Safety Toolbox.

Therapists

Most therapy training programs require individuals who want to become mental health professionals to undergo therapy themselves. There are several underlying reasons.

If your therapist has experienced being the client, she has worked on her own issues. More importantly, she knows what it's like to be the client and has firsthand knowledge of what practices work and which ones do not. She's literally been in your seat.

Therapy offers a mental health professional a safe space to dive into personal issues. This helps the future therapist become familiar with things that could become a problem in practice if not addressed. Blind spots and triggers can be uncovered and resolved.

A therapist who has a therapist is an example of someone who believes therapy works, reducing the stigma about getting help for mental health issues.

A therapist who faces an ethical issue and who is already in therapy has a built-in mentor to discuss issues and might avoid a potentially harmful situation.

Therapy can also prevent burnout or compassion fatigue. Being in therapy helps a therapist deal with the trauma that can come from dealing with other people's traumatic experiences and/or histories of abuse. The same therapies they offer us can help them form coping skills to deal with whatever arises in their mental health professional work.

An effective therapist must have self-knowledge and a willingness to self-reflect. Therapy builds and improves those skills.

Meditation Teachers

For many of the same reasons it's wise for a therapist to have a therapist, a meditation teacher can also use a wise consultant—their own teacher—to guide them on this path.

The first and foremost reason is ethics. Leaders need guardrails. This is true of therapists, but even more so with meditation teachers, since teachers and students may retreat together for long periods, including overnight stays. There's also the guru factor, the way in which a teacher can lose perspective and may act out improperly, believing they are above reproach. Teachers must guard against their own egos.

Because a small percentage of people who meditate experience unhelpful side effects, it's important to have resources on which to rely if this occurs. If you have a past history of trauma, be sure your teacher is trained in trauma and is interested in how your meditation is going. A trained teacher can help you avoid unwanted side effects or work through them with as little difficulty as possible.

If you experience disturbing or emotionally disruptive symptoms, please see a mental health professional right away. Your meditation teacher and therapist can help you find additional appropriate resources.

Summary

When you're dealing with something as personal and powerful as your psyche—or perhaps the nature of consciousness—it's important to have a trustworthy, knowledgeable guide who understands what you're going through.

Those of us with mental health challenges tend to trust people who have been in our shoes or who can at least see our shoes! Having both a therapist and a meditation teacher will allow you to build that trust. You want the person on whom you rely to have resources and employ safeguards. You want them to have their own "check engine light" in the same way they provide one for you. You can't trust someone who flies blind.

In the next chapter, I'll talk about how you might already be accidentally meditating during your movement practice, and possibly throughout your day.

CHAPTER 18

YOU MIGHT ALREADY BE DOING IT

Accidental Meditation

Long before you knew about or tried movement meditation, if the conditions were right, you may have accidentally fallen into a state of mindful awareness. Meditation is a natural state some people experience without realizing that's what it is. You might exercise in part to achieve this calm, concentrated mind state. I know I do. Once you've experienced the pleasure and relief of conscious movement, the impact on the rest of your life becomes clear. When you drop resistance and become fully immersed in the present, that's meditation.

So, you exercise more. It motivates you. You might have experienced it while making art, playing music, being out in nature, traveling, or being with a loved one. And you might not have realized it's the meditative state you actually enjoy. Plus, you couldn't always make that mind state happen. Now that you know how to meditate while you move, you will be able to do it on purpose.

When you apply the movement meditation practices in this book, you are more likely to drop into that focused, calm state. More importantly, you will suffer less when you don't. You hope for the high but accept if it doesn't come. You learn to tolerate any unpleasantness inherent in the activity. The effort is worthy regardless of the outcome. Effort becomes the goal. No need to chase it, since chasing pushes it away.

Train your mind to appreciate this mind state, and you won't need to hope for accidental or peak meditative experiences. Create conditions which allow the mind to clear, focus, and grow wise. Appreciate these when they come, and enjoy the process regardless. Equanimity around such experiences is as important as the experience itself. This is skillful means.

Is an accidental mindful experience as meaningful as intentional meditation?

It depends on what you do with it. (You knew I would say that.) If you see it for what it is, fleeting and impermanent, and let it pass away as it wishes, then yes. But if you grasp after it, that only leads to more suffering.

You may also have had what's known as a peak experience—a momentary, random flash of insight. People reporting peak experiences note awareness of the connectedness of all things, the sense of self dropping away, and an abundant joy, all happening in a flash. Sounds lovely. And they don't last. In fact, after a peak experience, someone not trained in meditation, and especially someone not aware of the power of equanimity, may suffer greatly as they try to maintain or regain this state of consciousness.

People who meditate regularly may also have peak experiences. The difference is that they know what to do when it happens. You guessed it! Recycle this into the practice. Observe it with full attention and a calm mind. Appreciate it while it lasts. When it passes, let it go.

When I mentioned the idea of accidental meditation to an Olympic weight-lifter friend who also swims, she said, "Oh yes. The rhythmic movement of swimming might induce a meditative state."

I agreed that rhythmic movement can reset the nervous system and rewire the brain, switching off the stress alarm. This makes it calming. But that's not what I was talking about.

I suggested she might be accidentally meditating while lifting weights. "When you've got that bar over your head, you're probably focused and relaxed." I clarified that by "relaxed" I meant relaxed internally as well as physically—not slouched, holding tension equally, and not tensing any unnecessary muscles.

"I never thought of it that way," she said, but agreed with my assessment.

If, as part of your dance routine or yoga, you stare at a spot on the wall for focus, balance, or perspective, that's concentration that might lead to a focused, calm state. Similarly, listening to music with so much concentration that everything but the sound drops away is a meditative state.

Any activity that brings you fully into the present moment, whether you intend that or not, is meditative. This is good news. Meditation is a natural ability that goes along with being human. You already know how to do it. If you choose, develop it more.

Mindful or Self-Conscious?

Does mindful movement require self-consciousness?

At first, yes.

Your initial efforts to meditate while moving may feel clunky and slow. It might help to remember you have likely already experienced meditation. It's not foreign or exotic; it's entirely natural. Now you're just learning how to summon, use, and build the meditative state of mind.

Didn't your sport feel awkward at first? Anything that requires practice feels odd until you get the hang of it.

If you wish, start slowly with your movement meditation, choosing a short interval of time. Grow into this the same way you might with a physical fitness practice. Few people can bench press fifty pounds the first time they try. Play with it and see how your awareness waxes and wanes. Do your best to stay present, pulling your mind back to your chosen object of meditation if it roams. Observe how the intensity of the exercise impacts the mindfulness.

During your first forays into mindful movement practice, the mind may wander and skitter. In the midst of intense exercise, the mind may calm. It must focus on what you're doing and cannot jump around.

What about my friend who thought swimming was her mindful state? It no doubt is. But her Olympic weight lifting is more likely to induce a spontaneous meditative mind state because the inherent risks ratchet up the focus. She is deep in concentration with that barbell above her head.

With practice, mindful movement becomes a working part of the way you do things. Practice turns into your usual mode. Self-consciousness drops away. You no longer need to practice being mindful; you are mindful. This is what it means to lose yourself in the activity or to be in the zone. Movement and mindfulness become automatic. There's no *you* moving; there's only motion.

Summary

The states of mind that result from meditation may sound familiar and may be one of the reasons you enjoy your movement form. Meditation is a natural mind state. You might have been meditating or had peak experiences by accident. Now that you know how to meditate, create conditions for this to happen, and know what to do when it does. Do it on purpose!

Next, let's look at how surrounding yourself with people who also practice can benefit you. You may already experience this in a movement community. You can find the same benefits in a meditation community.

CHAPTER 19

FIND YOUR FELLOWSHIP

The Benefits of Community

The annual running of the Emerald City race in Dublin, Ohio, fell on my birthday. For the occasion, I donned my green, glittered Bolder Athletic Wear running skirt and matching "6run4" top (central Ohio is in the "614" area code). When I arrived, one running friend greeted me with a birthday tiara while another pinned an "It's My Birthday" sash across my chest.

Along the route, nearly every runner or walker, whether I knew them or not, sang out "Happy Birthday!" A sense of belonging warmed my heart. When central Ohio's August heat and the fatigue of running six miles made it difficult, those positive body sensations helped me continue. I like to think runners share a special bond, stronger and better than that of other groups, but I doubt we're unique. All humans crave kinship. If we look, we can find it.

Community support is beyond important. At times, it's essential. There might be peer pressure, but there is also the camaraderie of being with like-minded people who follow the same approach. Your chosen movement form probably has such a fellowship. It might be the racquet club or golf league or, like mine, the running group. This is essentially our *sangha*.

Reasons to participate in a group include:

1. *Peer pressure and accountability*. Oh! Your friends are working out today. Shouldn't you be with them? That voice in your head might be your best cheerleader. Sure, it's FOMO ("fear of missing out"), but FOMO gets the job done. Always watch for the tendency for this feeling to pull that instrument string too tight. Awareness keeps you on the middle way.

2. *Cross-pollination*. You don't necessarily mean to learn things in your group. That might not be why you joined, but research shows that you become like your closest group of friends. You do what they do and get what they've got. If you want freedom from suffering, why not hang around with people doing the practice that frees them from suffering?

3. *Feedback*. A group often includes members of various levels. If you're new, you will get answers to questions, learn new things, and try things you might not on your own.

4. *Fights loneliness*. Loneliness is an epidemic in the United States and many other developed countries. Countless studies have shown the dangers, both physical and mental, of isolation. A group not only helps you combat your own loneliness, but your presence may help someone else.

With meditation, it doesn't matter if it is in person or virtual. A 2021 study reported in the *Clinical Social Work Journal* about group versus solitary meditation showed an increased benefit in sitting with others, even if the group practice was virtual. The study concluded that virtual group sessions would help during the pandemic when in-person sessions weren't available, and could be of use to populations not likely to go to in-person settings due to personal issues or lack of access.[71] Sangha is sangha even if it's in the "Hollywood Squares" virtual reality we learned to use during the pandemic.

You may have already experienced the power of exercising with others. In *The Practice of Groundedness*, author Brad Stulberg recommends what he calls *Deep Community*. "Exercising with other people promotes connection and belonging."[72] There are several reasons why this is so.

First, as a species, we are hardwired to find joy in group movement. "Synchrony with others" is what Stulberg calls it, and he explains how it dates back to the evolutionary advantage of the kind of cooperation needed to hunt in groups.

Second, the affection and bonding that happens in group activity releases happy brain chemicals, including endorphins and oxytocin.

Third, the rituals inherent in many exercise activities—the group photo, the group warm-up, posting a photo of your medal on social media, a collective breakfast after the run, or speed work done together—create an "identity fusion" (Stulberg), which is "feeling connected to and part of something larger than oneself."[73] This is why some people run, climb stairs, or do challenges for charity. Being part of a greater whole is intrinsically positive.

Fourth, group activity builds trust, especially if it involves facing challenges together. Your confidence in the other people in the group grows. Doing hard things is vulnerable. You might fail, but if you're in the right group, others will cheer your efforts, And, when you succeed, they cheer your achievement. That "muscular bonding," building relationships while doing physically difficult things together, underlies rites of passage in many

---

71   Adam W. Hanley PhD, Vincent Dehili PhD, Deidre Krzanowski RN, Daniela Barou MSW, Natalie Lecy LCSW, QMHP, & Eric L. Garland PhD, "Effects of Video-Guided Group vs. Solitary Meditation on Mindfulness and Social Connectivity: A Pilot Study" *Clinical Social Work Journal* (2021). doi.org/10.1007/s10615-021-00812-0.

72   Brad Stulberg, *The Practice of Groundedness* (New York: Penguin Random House, 2021), 182.

73   Brad Stulberg, *The Practice of Groundedness*, 182.

organizations, including tribal cultures, the military, and, hey, even band camp! You haven't loved people until you've crawled on your hands and knees singing "Beautiful Ohio" while they shower you with shaving cream and toilet paper.

I'll add a fifth reason he didn't mention. After you've done an activity with a group for a while, a newer person is bound to ask you a question. You'll know the answer, not from studying (although that wouldn't hurt), but from your own experience. Suddenly, you realize you know a thing or two. Positive body sensations, baby!

Service Is the Secret

In many traditions, meditators vow to save all beings. That's a tall order. Maybe you can't save all beings, but you can make small efforts (gradual progress) to help others. That might help you feel better about movement practice. Consider giving back.

Compassion fosters a desire to help. Community is a place where service can happen. If someone is new, explain how the community works and cheer them on in their movement and meditation. That is all service, and it all counts.

You don't need to become a meditation teacher. But please do so if that interests you. That's how I got involved with Sage Institute. I already taught, so I decided to earn credentials, learn more, deepen my practice, and ensure I do more good than harm.

But even the simple act of telling someone how you combine movement with meditation can serve the people around you. Don't be overzealous, of course. Meditation, like recovery programs, draws participation more through attraction than promotion. Still, there is nothing wrong with sharing that you've found a process that helps you exist in a less painful, more joyful way.

Service can look many different ways. Help at an event. Volunteer at a competition. Teach young people how to do the sport you love. Donate money to a movement and meditation cause.

Service keeps you involved. You are present—you are in the activity, doing the thing, with people. It keeps your toe in the water, moving forward, being present.

It's also a great way to meet people and stave off loneliness. If you sign up to help renovate the meditation center (or the golf club or the dance studio), you won't be doing it alone. You show up on a Saturday morning, and someone is there to talk to about the practice you share. That common bond is a great glue.

Plus, if you feel the benefits of movement meditation, you want to keep it alive. You owe this debt to the people who shared it with you, but you can't pay it back. You can only share it with others; you pay it forward.

Not Your Typical Sangha

With movement meditation, unless you join a group that already practices this way, you might have to create your own group. And, even if you join a group that does movement meditation, they might not practice the mindful movement I have described. What to do?

You could join any group that does the same movement form you enjoy, even if no one in that group meditates. When you're with them, doing your chosen movement form together, silently infuse your movement with awareness and equanimity. Recycle any reactions. You can meditate anywhere and on anything.

Introduce the group to meditation. If you benefit from movement meditation and want to share, anyone interested may want to become involved. Share this book with anyone curious about movement meditation. Point them to its Resources section.

Find a group already practicing mindful movement meditation. Look for the term "mindfulness" in the title or description of a group, workshop, or class. Mindfulness has arrived on the scene. It's everywhere! Contact the instructor or group leader to inquire whether she offers the type of mindful movement explained in this book, or attend the first session and ask questions about what will be taught. Know what you're getting into.

Or start your own group! Social media and other connection websites make it easier than ever to connect with groups of like-minded people. Contact me for help. Or contact another meditation teacher. Make it clear you are not trained to teach meditation or lead a group. Hold space for a group to form, and provide some basic support for other people who want to transform their movement activity into a meditation practice.

Find an existing meditation group and invite others to begin to move during a separate movement meditation practice session. This way, you have the support of a teacher who might already be doing movement practice, but you are also giving back to their sangha by offering something new and different.

Or you may realize you don't need an in-person group with which to do the movement meditation practice. But you will want to be connected to some form of sangha so the support of other meditation practitioners will be available to you. Virtual sanghas across the world can provide accountability, structure, information, and resources you do not have on your own. Connection with a virtual sangha, even if you don't move with them, still offers the benefit of the group's collective wisdom and the teacher's expertise.

Here's what I do:

As an alumna of the Sage Institute for Creativity and Consciousness 200-hour meditation leader training program, I stay in touch with my teacher Sensei Sean Murphy and the community of students and teachers in that program. My regular meetings with Sean include discussions of my practice.

He asks how it's going, any problems I might be facing, and what techniques I'm using. That is my regular sangha.

I also continue learning from Shinzen Young. He offers several opportunities for interaction including a monthly "Ask-Me-Anything" which is offered to people who have studied with him in the past. I belong to the Shinzen Young Mindfulness Community and the Unified Mindfulness Private Group Coaching Facebook groups where I ask and answer questions.

I sometimes sit and walk with local mindfulness and Zen groups. I continue to attend retreats with Natalie Goldberg, who teaches sitting, walking, and writing practice meditation. Retreats and sitting days are a great way to be with people interested in movement meditation and to learn from a teacher with decades of her own deep practice.

Running coach Denny Krahe and I also talk about meditation. He doesn't call himself a meditator, but he meditates. I get clear talking to him and enjoy the support and camaraderie of his online community.

I study with ChiRunning instructors, many of whom do sitting meditation. ChiRunning also has an online community where we can share about movement meditation.

Finally, before I became a certified meditation leader and long before this book came out, I "sneaked" mindfulness into conversations both at group runs and in the online groups Marathoner in Training and Still I Run: Runners for Mental Health Awareness. Remember the woman who asked about meditation? I explained noticing my left foot. She laughed, then later told me she had found trying it helpful. People still tease me about my "left foot meditation," and I enjoy that gentle ribbing. They are paying attention.

Summary

With loneliness at epidemic levels, you owe it to yourself and your community to get involved. While it may not be easy to find a group, the support, companionship, and accountability will help you maintain a practice and deepen your joy for whatever movement you choose.

In the next chapter, I'll discuss the dreaded I's: illness and injury. No one wants either, but I'll explain how to use them to your benefit if they happen.

CHAPTER 20

ILLNESS, INJURY, AND "BAD" WORKOUTS

How to Enjoy a Bad Workout

Have you ever started a workout and something immediately went wrong? Your shoe was untied, you tripped and fell, you turned left when you should have turned right, you did the wrong pose in front of the entire class, or you were in a bad mood.

There's a "running" joke (see what I did there?) about how to run a marathon. You just put one foot in front of the other for a mile and do that for twenty-six miles, then again for 365 yards (0.2 miles).

But there's so much truth in that. A marathon is a loooong way. Just because I forgot to turn on my watch at the start (yes, I've done that) or because my friends left me at mile 4—I told them to do that; I had to go to the bathroom—that doesn't mean the whole race will be bad.

Don't let getting off to a bad start discourage you. A bad mood or mishap early in the workout need not become an outcome. Movement meditation practice teaches us that every moment is separate. Because each moment is separate, one bad moment need not color the next. We only create these connections in our minds.

If your workout continues to go badly, consider letting it be bad. Give up trying to make it better. Instead, get curious about what a bad workout feels like. Notice the thoughts that arise. Make "bad" your object of meditation. Adopting that letting go mindset (a.k.a., equanimity) can alter your overall state of mind. Especially in a sport that keeps score of who's winning, it's easy to let a number decide whether or not you're having a good or a bad workout. Of course, you want to do your best, but every workout will not be fabulous. Every workout can, however, be an opportunity to practice—grist for the mill.

Besides, you don't actually know how you did until the workout, race, match, or game is over. Release what just happened and be present with what is happening right now. That's the only place reality lives: now, in this moment. It's the only thing over which you have any modicum of control, and even that's actually questionable.

During the workout, pay attention to the object of meditation you have selected, not the score or the bad start. If you're in a group, feel the camaraderie. If you're outdoors, check out the scenery. Check your attitude. Can you find gratitude? Do you need to give yourself Metta?

Shift your mindset from a goal-oriented one to that of the student—open, eager, and without preconceptions. Workouts become learning experiences, ones you can use not to berate yourself, but to shift mindsets. When you aim to learn as much as you can about your chosen fitness activity, as opposed to only focusing on how well you did, it makes that workout and every future workout more enjoyable.

What does it mean to run well or play well anyway? Of course, most of us want to succeed; we like to win, make the podium, get an award. But even champions don't win everything. Everyone has the occasional off day. It's all part of the practice: grist, if you will. Now that you have begun to train your mind, focus from moment to moment. Become enamored with the process. Fall in love with it, and you will never have a bad workout again.

Good? Bad?

How do we know what's good or bad anyway? Who are we to judge? Here's one of my favorite stories:

> "A poor farmer's horse ran off into the country of the Barbarians.
> All his neighbors offered their condolences, but his father said,
> 'How do you know that this isn't good fortune?'
>
> After a few months, the horse returned with a Barbarian horse of
> excellent stock. All his neighbors offered their congratulations, but
> his father said, 'How do you know that this isn't a disaster?'
>
> The two horses bred, and the family became rich in fine horses.
> The farmer's son spent much of his time riding them. One day, he
> fell off and broke his hip bone. All his neighbors offered the farmer
> their condolences, but his father said, 'How do you know that this
> isn't good fortune?'
>
> Another year passed, and the Barbarians invaded the frontier. All
> the able-bodied young men were conscripted, and nine-tenths of
> them died in the war. The son was spared because of his injury.
>
> Thus, good fortune can be disaster and vice versa. Who can tell
> how events will be transformed?"
>
> —"The Huai Nan Tzu Tells a Story," from the *Tao Te Ching*,
> translated by Stephen Mitchell[74]

---

74   Laozi, *Tao Te Ching*. Trans. Stephen Mitchell. (New York: Harper Perennial, 1994).

If there is no good or bad, why do we judge our workouts? Have you ever had a breakup, lost a job, or had a setback that turned out to be one of the best things that could have happened? This is what we're talking about.

This philosophy echoes the motto, "The best meditation is the one you do." Apply that to everything. The best run is the one you run. The best dance is the one you do. The best game is the one you play. The best practice round is the one you do.

Our minds want to put things in boxes. They want safety. But often, we just don't know. What is true today may be put in an entirely different light by something tomorrow. Of course, we can celebrate and enjoy. Yet we cannot know if it is good or bad. A balanced mind is not caught off guard.

Turn It into an Opportunity

When you rely on a mode of exercise for your mental health and well-being, an illness or injury can throw you. Check any fitness magazine and you'll find a list of suggestions. These tips, often helpful, include: changing your perspective, journaling or keeping a diary, goal-setting for a new, smaller goal, focusing on the things you can control, finding a different hobby or outlet to focus on while you recover, putting your energy into rehabbing the injury, staying connected to community, staying positive, and practicing gratitude. The list might include breathing techniques (sometimes called "meditation") to calm you.

What if I can't calm down?

These popular fitness articles miss the true benefit of meditation and the opportunity an illness or injury offers. I know. I hear you groaning. Listen. You're injured or you're sick. You can't reverse that. Might as well make the best of it. You already know what I'm going to say.

Make it grist for your meditation mill.

Turn your awareness to the thoughts and body sensations that arise from the injury, to the pain itself, and the frustration. Do your best not to get lost in the stories your mind creates. Instead, notice the thoughts, the regrets, the worry, and the projections. "Why did I take that fire-jumping, barbed-wire wrestling, lion-taming challenge anyway?" Turn your awareness to those. Be willing to let go of any negative stories—release those fixed ideas of who you think you are or what you should have done. They change as you watch.

Do the same with an illness. The last time I was sick, it lasted a few weeks. I couldn't run, and it was tough. My mind asked, "When will I be well?" and, "When can I run again?" I let "don't know mind" become my practice, noticed my discomfort at not having answers, and did my best to relax around it.

Do your best.

A friend who suffers from migraines explained how, during her worst episodes, she cannot do any movement form. Despite years of meditation practice, when she tries to meditate through them, even while lying down, she experiences freak-out. The pain is too intense. Thoughts and body sensations come too quickly for her to stay mindful. She can dip her toe into awareness for a bit, but when the experience overwhelms her, she must zone out. I encouraged her to be gentle with herself and not to expect too much but to continue to try to practice during the episodes, and at other times, too. Any meditation she does will build her abilities. One day, she may find relief by meditating during her migraines.

When illness or injury strikes, infuse the thoughts and body sensations with the clarity of focus and the mind state of equanimity. Open with acceptance, and see what happens. Make that your new challenge. Instead of trying to distract yourself, turn toward. Turn toward. Turn toward.

Another Chance to Practice

Several years ago, I signed up for a half marathon in Maryland. I want to run a half marathon in each of the fifty states. During a trip to Washington, DC, I planned to drive to Baltimore for the half while Ed attended a conference in the Capital.

In the months before our trip, a local race chose my runner friend Deirdre Pifer's splendid design to adorn the medal. Our group was running it to support her artistic achievement.

On race day, I didn't listen to my body. I un-mindfully pushed too hard trying to catch another runner going up a hill. The popping sound my knee made turned my stomach as pain shot through my leg. "This can't be good." Walking became limping because I couldn't put full weight on my leg.

A visit to the doctor yielded a prescription for anti-inflammatory drugs and a diagnosis: a torn meniscus. My heart broke when that doctor, also a runner and a trainer for college sports teams as well as the medical director for our Columbus Marathon, told me my knee would take at least six weeks to heal. That Maryland race was out of the question.

Because I run as much for mental health as fitness, injuries cause more emotional pain than physical. The anguish of not being able to run for six weeks felt overwhelming. My mind, always tricky, built a story. "You'll gain fifty pounds. You'll lose all your fitness. You're an idiot for running so hard in a race that didn't count."

Plus, I was limping. Even walking hurt.

As I did my physical therapy exercises, I saw how the story my mind created was not true. No, I did not want to be injured. Yes, it hurt. Yes, I was disappointed not to be checking off the Maryland box on my fifty-state list. And yes, I knew I needed to rest and let it heal, which it eventually did.

And I knew what to do.

That injured knee gave me so many things to work with:

Physical pain. Walking became noticing the unpleasant body sensations that arose in my knee. It swelled. Ice hurt. Bending it hurt. I reacted badly to the anti-inflammatory medication my doctor prescribed and chose not to take opiates because of my history of addiction. Instead, I relied on meditation to manage the pain. I took the over-the-counter medicines and doubled down on practice.

Each physical sensation, big or small, around the experience became my object of meditation. I could hear Shinzen's voice. "Infuse experience with awareness and equanimity." Notice the sensation arising and passing away. What does it feel like? Does it move? Be inside the pain: Not thinking about the pain, but experiencing it from the inside—being fully inside my body.

I wanted to escape. Food helped for a bit, but not much. I don't drink alcohol. Caffeine makes me crazy; I didn't need a panic attack on top of this. Nothing was left except going fully into the physical pain. While I'm not ready to have dental work without Novocain the way Shinzen has, I learned to be present with intense pain.

Emotional pain. Disappointment set a deep, heavy weight in my belly and pushed downward on my shoulders. Anger burned; my throat flamed with it, and my stomach felt like a cauldron. The emotions resonated into my abdomen and moved and changed and morphed and shifted, offering me glimpses of impermanence.

Thoughts. Mine tend to come in from the right side of my mind, welling up and moving across from right to left, the opposite of reading a page. Thoughts taunted me about having been stupid to try to catch that runner. Others were words of self-pity. Why had this happened to me? I try to be careful. I also saw images: the hill I had been climbing when the knee popped. Visual images and auditory sensations. All of those things dragged me away from the present.

Finally, *who's injured?* Who was sensing this pain and confusion? Of course, it was "me," but none of it was permanent. It fluxed and flowed as I observed. Insight.

My job with each of these—physical pain, emotions, and thoughts—was the same. Notice the arising. Stay present. Bring my mind back when it wandered. Let the thoughts and body sensations do what they would. Notice what stays, changes, passes. Notice. Notice. Notice. Always with an openhanded spirit of equanimity. Letting experience do its dance.

Pain times resistance equals suffering. If I could drop the resistance, the pain would remain, but the suffering would be diminished.

Need Help? Get Help.

Learning to use illness and injury as objects of meditation is especially important for those of us who live with mental health conditions. When you rely on exercise as part of your survival tool kit, an injury that prevents being active and able to utilize that tool can cause a lot more disruption to you than to a person without mental health challenges.

In addition to meditation, during illness and injury you might need help from a mental health professional. You might need an increase in therapy sessions or medication to get you through the recovery.

Feel no shame for this.

Get through, and see what happens.

Does this sound contradictory? It is. On the one hand, meditation will help when nothing else does. But use all the tools at your disposal. Meditation cannot fix anything. It helps you see clearly what is happening and helps you withstand it.

Don't suffer if another remedy can help.

Summary

Now you have skills to help you on the road to both internal and external recovery.

Once you're able to work out again, let's talk about performance and how meditation helps with that.

CHAPTER 21

PERFORMANCE

Mindful Sports

> "If you want to change something, first increase your awareness
> of the way it is. Awareness itself is curative. Whatever helps to
> increase awareness of what is will promote learning; whatever
> hides or distorts awareness of what is will block
> or distort learning."[75]
> —W. Timothy Gallwey, *The Inner Game of Golf*

Let's not kid ourselves. We may think about becoming enlightened, but first we want to win the game. You might want more accurate, powerful serves, longer, straighter golf drives, the strength and coordination to nail that balance beam routine, or to lift heavier weights. Whatever you've chosen, chances are you hope to not only be at it for a long time, but to excel. It may be what drew you to movement in the first place. Improved performance is a fabulous, legitimate motivator. While I doubt that I'll ever qualify for the Boston Marathon, I still enjoy winning my age group from time to time.

---

75   W. Timothy Gallwey, *The Inner Game of Golf*, Random House (1998), p. 68.

Nearly every sports performance book I read while researching this book suggested mindfulness. Some authors included a full chapter or program. Others wove mindfulness throughout. While I didn't set out to write a performance book, if as a result of movement meditation your performance improves, as mine has, what a lovely byproduct.

Beware making enhancement the goal, as that could increase suffering. The way you approach and hold the goal matters more than what the goal itself. Goals are not inherently bad. Buddhism gets a bad reputation for being goalless, wandering, and aimless. Some of that reputation is earned. But within that is a seed of something truer.

Meditation is a "yes *and*" philosophy, a "this *and* that" way of being. It allows you to have a goal while also not having a goal. To reduce your suffering, focus more on the process than the result.

I would love to run faster and for longer distances. This desire can give rise to the pain of disappointment in my heart and belly as I watch runners with whom I used to compete leave me in the literal dust. But pushing too hard could lead to injury. As I age, I continue to train, do my best to accept the outcome, and turn any disappointment into another object of meditation. I work on form, focus, and relaxation in my body (external) as I notice the desire to win (internal).

Focus more on the process than the goal.

This is contrary to the "win" focused mindset offered by some sports performance coaches. Yes, we want to succeed. We will work for it. We will be disappointed if we don't do well. And we will suffer less by holding that desire to succeed and any disappointments loosely. Turn more attention to what's happening in this moment. Fill that with equanimity and reduce the potential suffering.

Know Thyself

Performance coach Gary Mack, author of *Mind Gym: An Athlete's Guide to Inner Excellence*, explains that each athlete is an individual. He urges his athletes to "know your numbers" for optimal performance and "recognize your early warning signs."[76]

He explains:

> "Under stress, some people are cardiac responders—their heart rate goes up. Some are skin responders—they begin to perspire. Others begin to breathe rapidly, feel their stomachs lurch, or feel their neck and back muscles tensing. These are all physical early warning signs. Mentally, our minds start racing. A little voice begins whispering negative thoughts."
>
> —Gary Mack[77]

What better way to "know your numbers" and "recognize your early warning signs" than mindfulness? Once you begin to practice movement meditation regularly, you will become more familiar with the way you respond to stress. You will learn to back off when you experience your early warning signs and push when it is appropriate. You will feel it in your body and hear thoughts in your mind. You will know yourself and be able to adjust accordingly.

Stress and Recovery

The training pattern of most schedules for a long race includes several weeks of build-up followed by a "fall back" in which mileage is reduced. This fall back follows the principle of stress and recovery. Exercise stresses

---

76 Gary Mack, *The Mind Gym: An Athlete's Guide to Inner Excellence*, (New York: McGraw-Hill, 2001), p. 30.

77 Gary Mack, *The Mind Gym*, p. 31.

the muscles. Rest allows them to recover. During the recovery, muscles rebuild stronger than before.

The corollary in meditation is regular practice interspersed with intense retreats. Take a similar approach to your movement meditation practice. At first, you may find it difficult to even remember to practice while you are exercising. Any day you practice is a good one. Challenge yourself to a longer session during a longer workout. Or register for a retreat. Let that strengthen your mind muscles. After, return to your workouts with heightened awareness and equanimity.

Summary

Enjoy any performance benefits, but focus on the process rather than the goal; this is easier said than done, but worth it. Here's another riddle to ponder: *There is no path, and you're on it.* This moment is what counts.

In this next (and final) chapter, I'll bid you adieu until we meet again.

CHAPTER 22

SEE YOU ON THE "PATH"

Eagle Up

My feet hurt: not both of them, and not the entire foot. Mostly just the bottom of my right foot, the one that bears more weight because of that congenital "wonky ankle" defect.

I'd been running and walking for nine hours along the wooded tow path of the Ohio Erie Canal in northeastern Ohio, twenty-nine miles into Eagle Up, my first ultramarathon. My goal was thirty-one miles and change, a "50k."

It was hot. The leaves of lush deciduous trees hung heavy in the June humidity. That foot, swollen and sweat-soaked, throbbed. I knew from thousands of miles, a decade of experience, and prior consultations with trusted medical professionals that I was in no permanent danger. Despite the story my mind created—"You're going to die, and even if you don't, you won't be able to walk when this is over"—I probably just had bruised toes.

As I slowed, other runners and walkers passed. I wanted it to be over. I wanted to be done.

I was close, but not done.

I'd easily meditated during most of the race, completing each five-mile loop at my own pace, running solo except for one lovely loop shared with my friend, Deirdre.

At the beginning of the race, I had used a broad focus of awareness, allowing my mind to land on what it wanted and occasionally drilling awareness into any visual sensation that arose. Now, a very specific sensation called: the pain in my right foot.

To distract myself, I sang "Amazing Grace." I said my favorite lawyer joke out loud—a long one that has three parts. I tried to zone out.

Nothing worked. That pulsing foot demanded all of my attention.

Amid this struggle, a calm, quiet thought arose: "This is the only time you will ever be two miles from finishing your first ultramarathon. Be where you are. Let this be."

Tears mixed with sweat burned my eyes.

To get out of the woods and back to the campground where the finish line beckoned, I had only one choice: Keep walking. I was not going to DNF ("did not finish") this race when I was so close to being done.

In response, my mind began to chant familiar refrains: "Who do you think you are? Why did you think you could do this? You're going to die."

My throat closed. The green arch of trees that felt so welcoming earlier in the day seemed certain to swallow me. I stopped and shook my head to repel the thoughts as if they were flies. My heart pounded.

Then, I remembered another Shinzen saying, *"Escape into discomfort."*[78]

Time to change tactics.

---

[78] Shinzen Young, "Escape Into Discomfort / My Interview with Shinzen Young," interview by Noah Rasheta, *Secular Buddhism Podcast*, November 19, 2017. secularbuddhism. com/shinzen-young.

As I began to walk again, I turned my full attention to the bottom of that right foot, opening to the pain and letting the ache flood me. It felt solid, like a hard, heavy, burning brick.

I could stay present with the pain for only a few seconds before I hit freak-out. I tensed and tried to point my mind toward anything else: the green trees, my sweaty body, those churning thoughts.

But shifting the focus was useless. That pain demanded my full attention. Back into the sensations of that right foot I went.

I zoomed my focus closer into that sore foot and got curious. Gradually, the sensations began to shift. The solid block softened, turning to undulating goo. While still extremely unpleasant, it now moved and flowed. I let it expand and contract. And I kept moving too.

Now that I'd committed to escaping *into* the discomfort, time began to flow as well. Eventually, the once endless trail opened to the street which led to the campground. Continuing to return my focus to that foot again and again, I circumnavigated the camp's edge, completed the one-mile out-and-back required for the 50k course, and crossed the finish line.

But when I stepped on the timing mat, I stumbled. A volunteer rushed over and invited me to sit on a bench. I'd been in motion for ten hours. Stopping disoriented me. Finish lines are often a mix of happiness, sadness, and confusion—amazing and slightly anticlimactic. What the heck had just happened?

"Am I really done?" I asked.

The volunteer nodded and called to Eric, the race director, who brought over a 50k medal, hung it around my neck, and hugged me. "Congratulations," he said.

With his words, joy arose. I could have kissed him.

And yes, my foot still hurt. Everything hurt! But I was not suffering. The meditation had done its job.

Accidental Mental Health Advocate

Depression Hates a Moving Target turned me into an accidental mental health advocate. Once I realized my story helped others, I embraced the role. When I share how running helps anxiety, depression, paranoia, and the mood swings that come from bipolar disorder, people get it.

And even though I mentioned meditation many times in that first book, I didn't explain how I used it with movement. It seemed obvious. It wasn't. I already had the tools of practice, awareness, and mindfulness in the tool kit, helping me stay alive. I hope this book makes that clear.

Of course, you don't need a mental health diagnosis to move mindfully. Everyone deserves wellness and mental health care, especially at this time on our planet. And nearly anyone can meditate, regardless of their mental health status. We're all on a continuum, and even on that we shift. No one is fully well or healthy every hour of every day.

While I have a soft spot in my heart for those with difficult mental health challenges and for whom life is harder than for others, we all have similar mental processes. Challenges are matters of degree. Mindful movement works for most of these issues, no matter where you are on that continuum.

Then, You Walk Back to the Car

After I crossed the finish line of that first ultramarathon, stunned by heat, pain, and accomplishment, and then sat down on that nearby bench, emotions flooded my body. My bruised, swollen toes radiated pain up my legs. My heart beamed joy and gratitude across my chest. I also felt a little numb.

Yes, I had finished the race, met the goal, done the thing. But I wasn't really done. I had to get back to my car.

Once I felt steady enough to walk, I stood, made my way to our campsite where Ed and my friends who had already finished were waiting, and sank into a chair. Later, we walked to the car and drove away.

That's the way it is. This race, match, game, recital, contest, workout will end. And then, you too will walk back to your car. Later, you'll return to your home court, your nearby trail, your neighborhood studio, or the local links to practice again—over and over and over. Hopefully with joy, and for a very long time.

I'll see you on the path.

May you be well.

May you be peaceful.

May you be happy.

May no harm come to you.

May you be free from suffering.

May you live with comfort and ease.

Welcome to the Sangha.

AN INVITATION
AND A REQUEST

I sincerely hope you found this book helpful. Like most writers, I love to connect with readers. Consider this your invitation to hop into my Facebook Group: Mind, Mood, and Movement. Post your own movement meditation experiences (or any life lessons) on my Facebook page at www.facebook.com/nitasweeneyauthor/ or tag me on your favorite social media channel.

As a special bonus, download the "Your Turn Exercises" booklet gratis at www.nitasweeney.com. You'll also find my free ebook, *Three Tools for a Happier, Healthier Mind*, as well as guided meditations.

I welcome all feedback. If you like the book, please let me know (via email at nita@nitasweeney.com) and post a positive review on Amazon and Goodreads. If you didn't like it, I'm open to hearing that as well, but let's keep it between us. ;-)

Thank you for reading!

RESOURCES

The Formula:

"Infuse your experience with awareness and equanimity."

—Shinzen Young

Definitions:

Experience: thoughts and body sensations

Body Sensations (the 5 sense gates): breath, felt sense (touch), sight, sound, taste, smell

Thoughts (the sixth sense gate): auditory or visual

Awareness (focus or concentration): one-pointed, diffuse, scanning, or free-floating

Equanimity: an inner condition developed through practicing all of the above with right intention

Steps to Make any Move a Meditation

0. Set an intention.

1. Choose a form of movement.

2. Choose an interval or period of time.

3. Choose an aspect of experience (i.e., an object of meditation).

4. Begin the movement practice. As you move, place your awareness on the object you have chosen.

5. When your mind wanders, gently bring your attention back to your chosen object of meditation.

6. Do all of this gently, with no strain and no self-judgment. Be curious and open, interested and aware.

7. If your body and/or mind responds, acknowledge that response and then either return to your original object of meditation or intentionally make the response your new object of meditation.

8. If you forget this, contact a qualified teacher who will help you remember.

Shinzen's Five Axioms

In one of his most quoted talks, Shinzen summarized his approach to mindfulness meditation:

"There are Five Axioms (or Five Basic Assumptions) that underlie mindfulness as I would teach it, that—when implemented—lead to not logical conclusions but to experiential developments within a person:

1. Concentration: It is better to have the ability to focus on what one deems relevant and whenever one wants than to lack that ability.

2. Sensory clarity: It is better to be sensorially clear about what's going on than to be sensorially muddled.

3. Equanimity: It is good to be able to not fight with yourself.

4. Recycle the reaction: If, as the result of applying the first three axioms, one experiences heavenly, hellish, or bizarre phenomena, then simply reapply to these reactions the first three axioms.

5. If you forget the first four axioms, have the contact information of a competent guide, call them, and they will remind you of the first four axioms."[79]

—Shinzen Young

---

79 Shinzen Young, "Five Basic Assumptions in Mindfulness Practice." youtu.be/
    s1QWEk9c0D4.

ACKNOWLEDGMENTS

On the many days writing this book felt impossible, I brought to mind the countless people who contributed. Positive sensations flooded my body as visual thoughts of their faces and auditory thoughts of their voices buoyed me. "Thank you" doesn't come close to repaying them. To those I failed to mention, know you're in my heart regardless. Deep bows to:

Natalie Goldberg for her wise teachings, especially the "Warning" in *Thunder and Lightning*. Shinzen Young for smart, witty meditation instruction that normalizes geeking out about mindfulness, and especially for that turning point phone conversation. Bhante Gunaratana for decades of compassionate instruction. Marcia Rose for kind, steadfast teaching. Lama Jacqueline Mandell for gentle, affirming, clear guidance to this eager, new, confused student. Sage Institute for Creativity & Consciousness for showing me how to step into the world in a new (ancient) way.

Sean Tetsudo Murphy, Sensei, for suggesting revisions that I resisted and that were exactly what the book needed. Tania Casselle for asking important, difficult questions. Donna Poland and Kae Denino for kind, aggravating, accurate suggestions. Alan Hirsch for attending to the details.

Katherine and Danny Dreyer for founding ChiRunning, Doug Dapo and Jeanette Bays for teaching me the specifics, and new ChiRunning owners Harrison Wong, Constanza Lisdero, Lisa Pozzoni, Sarah Richardson, and Vince Vaccaro for carrying the torch forward.

Daron Larson, Jeff Sinclair, Alan Francis, Patrick Dement, Brad Constable, Jim Smith, Pez Owen, Victor Cotea, W. T. S. Tarver, Theodora Hinkle, Andrew McMillan, Patricia Houser, Suzie Loveday, Juan Samuel Sangüesa Massiel, Kika Cicmanec, and other members of the Shinzen Young Mindfulness Community Facebook group. Each mindful movement meditation example you offered confirmed my mission.

The many members of Marathoner in Training, Still I Run: Runners for Mental Health Awareness board and community, and the Still I Run Grove City Chapter for so much it would fill another book.

Wall Street Journal reporter Ellen Gamerman for including this book in a roundup that brought exercise as meditation to the attention of a larger cross-section of readers. The Greater Columbus Arts Council and Ohio Arts Council for financial support that helped me complete this book.

The staff of the Market District Giant Eagle, especially Tim, Joy, Anita, Collyn, Stephen, Mani, George, Glorianne, Robin, and Tony, for letting me hold down a community room table for hours at a time until the pandemic drove me out. Colin Gawel, Tony, and the rest of the Colin's Coffee gang for McRoy sandwiches, sleepy mudshots, and for not yawning (openly) when I once again insisted on telling you the latest news about my books. Columbus Metropolitan Library staff, especially at the Hilliard, Hilltop, Karl Road, Main, Dublin and Whetstone branches for the quiet and study rooms, Joe and Bill at Main for answering my Chicago Manual of Style and citation questions, Margaret at Whetstone for continuing to be a friendly, helpful fan, and Brenna at Dublin for the air hugs. The staff at Best Western Hilliard Mill Run, especially Chris, for not looking at me funny when I only wanted to rent a room from 11 a.m. to 10 p.m. The staff at Hyatt Place Dublin for early check-in, late checkout, and unlimited decaf coffee.

Members of the "Mind, Mood, and Movement" and "The Writer's Mind" Facebook groups, for positive feedback on my mindful, mental health, and movement experiments, for embracing the unicorns, and for continuing to cheer long after the self-promo got boring. Subscribers to "Nita's News," my email newsletter, for their friendly replies and suggestions.

The ladies of Writer's Night Out, especially Shannon Jackson Arnold, Shirley Hyatt, Pat Snyder, Lora Fish, and Candace Hartzler, for support, generosity, wise counsel, and laughter. The Writeth-On tribe, especially Marie Radanovich, Mitsy Rayburn, Pat Snyder, Lora Fish, Shirley Hyatt, Joy Schroeder, Cheryl Peterson, Sharon Mast, Sally Stamper, and Karen Burry. Thank you for loving wild turkeys and our not-so-top-secret writing retreat as much as I do. And thank you to the rangers and staff at Columbus and Franklin County Metroparks for providing us with a safe space to create, eat, chat, and nap. Becca Syme, Susan Bischoff, Krystal Shannan, and the Better Faster Academy staff and members for affirming my Strengths, explaining why I struggle to write in my house, and showing me it's safe to shine. The remaining stalwarts on the Shutupandwrite loop. Thank you for staying around. And Lita Kurth for lending an ear.

Janice George, Beth Scherer, Dr. Julie Guthrie. Dr. Darrin Bright, and Dr. Rich Davis, the backbone of my physical and mental health team. The church basement, folding chair, and coffee pot people for helping me stay on the planet. Kim Watton for "that" social media post.

Scott Edelstein for guidance and suggestions, and for remaining calm when I wasn't.

Brenda Knight, Associate Publisher at Mango Publishing Group (a.k.a., my fairy godmother), without whose care and wrangling this book would not exist. May she continue to wave her magic wand for many years to come. Meloni Williams for patient editorial suggestions. And the entire team at Mango Publishing, some of the kindest and hardest working people in the world, for everything they do to bring this and other splendid books into the world.

My family, especially my sister Amy, brother Jim, and sister-in-law Deanna, for sending memes, never doubting, and cheering me from near and far.

My current canine running companion, Scarlet (a.k.a., the pupperina), known on social media as the #ninetyninepercentgooddog, whose unconditional love is boundless (as long as I supply treats). And Morgan, a true Zen master, forever in our hearts.

Finally, Ed, my love, my friend, my alpha reader, my #onehundredpercentgoodhusband. Here's to many more "Adventures with Ed."

ABOUT THE AUTHOR

Whether she's writing a book, running an ultramarathon, speaking to a group of lawyers, or leading a meditation session, Nita Sweeney's mission is to help people heal their minds.

Ironically, Nita's own mind still periodically tries to kill her. Clinically diagnosed with bipolar disorder, anxiety, PTSD, and paranoia, Nita discovered that, in addition to therapy and medication, she needs movement, meditation, and writing to stay alive. This realization prompted her to share her story and offer these techniques to others.

A meditator for more than twenty-five years, Nita primarily studies with Shinzen Young and Sean Tetsudo Murphy, Sensei, but has also studied with Bhante Gunaratana, Marcia Rose, Lama Jacqueline Mandell, and others. Nita earned her meditation leader certificate from Sage Institute for Creativity and Consciousness in Taos, New Mexico.

Her first book, the running and mental health memoir, *Depression Hates a Moving Target: How Running with My Dog Brought Me Back from the Brink*, received the Dog Writers Association of America Maxwell Medallion for the Human Animal Bond and was a finalist for the Faulkner Award. Nita coauthored the writing journal *You Should Be Writing* with Brenda Knight. An early draft of this book, *Make Every Move a Meditation*, was an Award-Winning Finalist in the Health: Diet & Exercise category of the International Book Awards.

Nita earned a journalism degree from the E.W. Scripps School of Journalism at Ohio University, a law degree from the Ohio State University, and a Master of Fine Arts degree in creative writing from Goddard College. She served as the assistant to writing practice originator Natalie Goldberg for ten years and has taught writing and meditation for more than two decades.

Nita founded the groups Mind, Mood, and Movement to support well-being through meditation, exercise, and writing practice, and The Writer's Mind, to share using writing practice to produce publishable work. Nita also publishes "Nita's News" for readers interested in her work as well as the writing resource newsletter, Write Now Columbus. Her ebook, *Three Tools for a Happier, Healthier Mind*, is available at no cost on her website at nitasweeney.com.

Nita lives in central Ohio, USA, with her husband, Ed, and their yellow Labrador retriever, Scarlet.

INDEX

REFERENCES

Abrahams, Matthew. *"The Trauma Dharma: The First Do No Harm training program aims to make meditation safer, in part by recognizing its pitfalls."* Interview with Willoughby Britton. *Tricycle*, April 10, 2018. tricycle. org/trikedaily/trauma-meditation.

Baker, Douglas. *Five-Minute Mindfulness: Walking—Essays and Exercises for Mindfully Moving Through the World.* Fair Winds Press (2016).

"Brahmavihara." Accessed November, 2021. en.wikipedia.org/wiki/ Brahmavihara.

"Buddhism for Beginners: Four Noble Truths" *Tricycle.* tricycle.org/ beginners/buddhism/four-noble-truths.

"Buddhism for Beginners: Eight-Fold Path" *Tricycle.* tricycle.org/beginners/ buddhism/eightfold-path.

Clinical and Affective Neuroscience Laboratory at Brown University. *"Meditation Safety Toolbox."* www.brown.edu/research/labs/britton/ meditation-safety-toolbox.

Egoscue, Pete. *Pain Free: A Revolutionary Method for Stopping Chronic Pain.* Bantam (Updated 2021).

Fronsdal, Gil. *"Equanimity"* May 29th, 2004. www.insightmeditationcenter. org/books-articles/equanimity.

Fronsdal, Gil, and Sayadaw U Pandita. *"A Perfect Balance" Cultivating Equanimity. Tricycle*, Winter 2005. tricycle.org/magazine/perfect-balance.

Gallwey, W. Timothy. *The Inner Game of Golf*, Random House (1981).

Gallwey, W. Timothy. *The Inner Game of Tennis: The Classic Guide to the Mental Side of Peak Performance*. Random House (1997).

Gamerman, Ellen. "New Books on Better Workouts That Include Brain as Well as Body." *The Wall Street Journal*, Jan. 11, 2022. www.wsj.com/articles/best-books-2022-workout-fitness-11641905831.

Gindin, Matthew. "The Buddhist Roots of Hatha Yoga." *Tricycle*, Fall 2019. tricycle.org/magazine/is-yoga-buddhist.

Goldberg, Natalie. nataliegoldberg.com.

Goldberg, Natalie. *Writing Down the Bones*. Shambhala (1986).

Goldberg, Natalie. "Meet Your Life." Mountain Cloud Zen Center, March 18, 2021. www.mountaincloud.org/dharmatalk-meet-your-life.

Goleman, Daniel, and Richard Davison. *Altered Traits*. Penguin Random House (2018).

Gunaratana, (Ven. Henepola) Bhante. bhavanasociety.org.

Gunaratana, Ven. Henepola. *Mindfulness in Plain English*. Wisdom Publications (1993).

Hanh, Thich Nhat. "The Heart of the Matter: Thich Nhat Hanh answers three questions about our emotions." *Tricycle*, Winter 2009. tricycle.org/magazine/thich-nhat-hanh-emotions.

Harp, David. *Mindfulness to Go: How to Meditate When You're on the Move*. New Harbinger Publications, Inc. (2011).

Hanley, Adam W. PhD, Vincent Dehili PhD, Deidre Krzanowski RN, Daniela Barou MSW, Natalie Lecy LCSW, QMHP, & Eric L. Garland PhD, "Effects of Video-Guided Group vs. Solitary Meditation on Mindfulness and Social Connectivity: A Pilot Study." *Clinical Social Work Journal* (2021). doi.org/10.1007/s10615-021-00812-0.

Kabat-Zinn, Jon. *Wherever You Go There You Are.* Hachette Books (2005).

Kaufman, Keith A., Carol R. Glass, and Timothy R. Pineau, *Mindful Sport Performance Enhancement: Mental Training for Athletes and Coaches.* American Psychological Association (2018).

Laozi, *Tao Te Ching.* Translated by Stephen Mitchell. New York: Harper Perennial, 1994.

Mack, Gary (with David Casstevens). *Mind Gym: An Athlete's Guide to Inner Excellence.* McGraw-Hill (2001).

Mandell, Jacqueline, Lama. www.samdenling.org/teachers.

Mitchell, Stephen. "The Huai Nan Tzu Tells a Story," Translated from *Tao Te Ching.*

Murphy, Sean Tetsudo, Sensei. www.murphyzen.com/bio.htm.

Murphy, Sean, Tetsudo, Sensei. *One Bird, One Stone: 108 Zen Stories.* Renaissance Books (2002).

Naumann, Robert K., Janie M. Ondracek, Samuel Reiter, Mark Shein-Idelson, Maria Antonietta Tosches, Tracy M. Yamawaki, and Gilles Laurent. "The reptilian brain," (2015 April 20). www.ncbi.nlm.nih.gov/pmc/articles/PMC4406946.

Orsillo, Susan M. PhD, and Lizabeth Roemer PhD. *The Mindful Way through Anxiety: Break Free from Chronic Worry and Reclaim Your Life.* Guilford (2011).

Parent, Joseph. *Zen Golf, Mastering the Mental Game* (2002).

Poole, Steven. *"The big idea: does practice make perfect?"* The Guardian, Monday, October 4, 2021. www.theguardian.com/books/2021/oct/04/does-practice-make-perfect.

Ratey, John J. *Spark: The Revolutionary New Science of Exercise and the Brain.* Little, Brown and Company (2008).

Riggs, Benjamin. "Everything the Buddha Ever Taught in 2 Words," *Elephant Journal*, May 12, 2014. www.elephantjournal.com/2014/05/everything-the-buddha-ever-taught-in-2-words.

Russell, Tamara, MSc, PhD, DClinPsych. *Mindfulness in Motion: a happier, healthier life through body-centered meditation.* Watkins (2015).

Sachter, Lawson, Sunya Kjolhede. "The Mind's Dragons: Deep practice mobilizes powerful healing energies—and stirs repressed forces that lie in our subconscious." *Tricycle* (Winter 2018). tricycle.org/magazine/the-minds-dragons.

Sarno, John, MD. *Mind Over Back Pain. A Radically New Approach to the Diagnosis and Treatment of Back Pain.* Berkley (1999).

Segal, Zindel V, John D Teasdale, Mark J. Williams. *Mindfulness-Based Cognitive Therapy for Depression.* Guilford (2002).

Seppala, Emma PhD. "18 Science-Backed Reasons to Try Loving-Kindness Meditation" *Psychology Today*, September 15, 2014.

Sheehan, Dr. George. "Did I Win?" (1993). www.georgesheehan.com/essays/did-i-win.

Shinzen Young Mindfulness Community Facebook Group. www.facebook.com/groups/shinzenyoungmindfulnesscommunity.

Shy, Yael. "Five Practices for Your Daily Commute: How to live in the moment when you're on the go." *Tricycle*, March 19, 2018. tricycle.org/trikedaily/practice-daily-commute.

Snyder, Gary. *The Practice of the Wild.* Berkeley: Counterpoint Press (2010).

Storr, Will. "The Brain's Miracle Superpowers of Self-Improvement." BBC. com, November 24, 2015. www.bbc.com/future/article/20151123-the-brains-miracle-superpowers-of-self-improvement.

Stulberg, Brad. *The Practice of Groundedness: A Transformative Path to Success That Feeds—Not Crushes—Your Soul.* Portfolio (2021).

Sweeney, Nita. "Bibliography for 'No Time to Meditate? Try a 'Micro-hit' of Mindfulness.'" July 2021. nitasweeney.com/2021/07/bibliography-for-no-time-to-meditate-try-a-micro-hit-of-mindfulness.

Unified Mindfulness. unifiedmindfulness.com.

Unified Mindfulness Wiki. unifiedmindfulness.com/wiki/index.php

"What the 'Finger Pointing to the Moon' analogy really means— from Zen Buddhism, the Buddha in the Shurangama Sutra'" essenceofbuddhism.wordpress.com/2016/04/19/what-the-finger-pointing-to-the-moon-analogy-really-means-from-zen-buddhism-the-buddha-in-the-shurangama-sutra.

Young, Shinzen. shinzen.org.

Young, Shinzen. "An Outline of Practice" May 2014, updated Aug 2016. www.shinzen.org/an-outline-of-practice.

Young, Shinzen. "What to Expect and Do After a Mindfulness Retreat ~ Shinzen Young (transcript)" unifiedmindfulness.com/wiki/index. php/What_to_Expect_and_Do_After_a_Mindfulness_Retreat_~_ Shinzen_Young_(transcript).

Young, Shinzen, "A.D.D. & the 'Do Nothing' Technique." www.youtube. com/watch?v=YNV6Y_JlhoA&t=1s.

Young, Shinzen. "Do Nothing" Meditation. www.youtube.com/ watch?v=cZ6cdIaUZCA.

Young, Shinzen Young. "Do Nothing" Meditation transcript.
    unifiedmindfulness.com/wiki/index.php/%22Do_Nothing%22_
    Meditation_.

Young, Shinzen. "Five Basic Assumptions in Mindfulness Practice" Nov 27,
    2009. www.youtube.com/watch?v=61QWEk9c0D4.

Young, Shinzen. "Purpose and Method of Vipassana Meditation" created
    November 29, 2010, modified December 7, 2016. www.shinzen.org/
    wp-content/uploads/2016/12/art_purpose.pdf.

Young, Shinzen. "The Power of Gone." November 6, 2015. www.shinzen.
    org/wp-content/uploads/2016/12/art_PowerofGone.pdf.

Young, Shinzen, "Natural Pain Relief." December 7, 2016. www.shinzen.org/
    wp-content/uploads/2016/12/art_synopsis-pain.pdf.

Young, Shinzen. *Natural Pain Relief,* audio CD. Boulder: Sounds True (2011).

Young, Shinzen. "Meditation: Escaping into Life—An Interview with
    Shinzen Young by Michael Toms." December 7, 2016. www.shinzen.
    org/wp-content/uploads/2016/12/art_escape.pdf.

Young, Shinzen. "Escape Into Discomfort / My Interview with Shinzen
    Young." Interview by Noah Rasheta, *Secular Buddhism Podcast,*
    November 19, 2017. secularbuddhism.com/shinzen-young.

Zeis, Patrick. "30 Evidence-Based Health Benefits of Meditation." May
    4, 2017. balancedachievement.com/areas-of-life/benefits-of-
    meditation.

Mango Publishing, established in 2014, publishes an eclectic list of books by diverse authors—both new and established voices—on topics ranging from business, personal growth, women's empowerment, LGBTQ studies, health, and spirituality to history, popular culture, time management, decluttering, lifestyle, mental wellness, aging, and sustainable living. We were recently named 2019 *and* 2020's #1 fastest-growing independent publisher by *Publishers Weekly*. Our success is driven by our main goal, which is to publish high-quality books that will entertain readers as well as make a positive difference in their lives.

Our readers are our most important resource; we value your input, suggestions, and ideas. We'd love to hear from you—after all, we are publishing books for you!

Please stay in touch with us and follow us at:

Facebook: Mango Publishing

Twitter: @MangoPublishing

Instagram: @MangoPublishing

LinkedIn: Mango Publishing

Pinterest: Mango Publishing

Newsletter: mangopublishinggroup.com/newsletter

Join us on Mango's journey to reinvent publishing, one book at a time.

CPSIA information can be obtained
at www.ICGtesting.com
Printed in the USA
LVHW031211140822
725846LV00006B/8